VALUE
SELLING

VALUE SELLING

Louis De Rose

AMERICAN MANAGEMENT ASSOCIATION

This book is available at a special
discount when ordered in bulk quantities.
For information, contact Special Sales Department,
AMACOM, a division of American Management Association,
135 West 50th Street, New York, NY 10020.

This publication is designed to provide accurate and authoritative information in
regard to the subject matter covered. It is sold with the understanding that the
publisher is not engaged in rendering legal, accounting, or other professional service.
If legal advice or other expert assistance is required, the services of a competent
professional person should be sought.

Library of Congress Cataloging-in-Publication Data

De Rose, Louis.
    Value selling / Louis De Rose.
    p. cm.
    Includes index.
    ISBN 0-8144-5975-7
      1. Selling. 2. Industrial procurement. I. Title. II. Title:
Value selling.
HF5438.25.D4   1989   89-45448
658.8'04--dc20   CIP

Printing number

10 9 8 7 6 5 4 3 2 1

Contents

Introduction   *vii*

1 Value and Its Meaning to the Industrial Customer   *1*
2 Buying Influences and Their Value Perceptions   *12*
3 The Meaning of Cost and the Relationship of Cost
   to Value   *27*
4 Identifying and Influencing Customer Requirements   *53*
5 The Value Selling Strategy Checklist   *71*
6 The Value Selling Presentation   *90*
7 Handling Objections, Complaints, and Changes   *109*
8 Establishing Credibility in Value Selling   *139*
9 Negotiating for Value   *171*

Epilogue   *211*

Index   *215*

Introduction

A basic requirement for all effective selling is a realistic concept of how and why markets and customers buy. *Value Selling* is a direct result of more than thirty years of experience in advising and training major corporations in their buying philosophies and practices. It is also the result of comparable time spent with marketing and sales people who seek to reach and sell to industrial, commercial, and institutional markets.

The common objective I have pursued with both buyers and sellers is an understanding of the concept *value*. Although it is one of the most frequently used words in the business vocabulary, we poorly define it. We use the term to describe some desirable or worthwhile standard for a product or service, or a fair and reasonable price for it. In either case, our use of the word is vague and tends to encourage competitive comparison on price alone.

Value is "the satisfaction of customer requirements at the lowest total cost in use." Like beauty, value is in the eye of the beholder, for it is perceived by the customer as he knows, understands, believes, or even feels his requirements to be. But value is realized only when those requirements—no matter how perceived—are satisfied at least total cost. That cost includes not only the initial price, which could be the only cost the customer acknowledges, but the costs subsequent to purchase, such as the costs of handling, inspecting, using, maintaining, repairing, and replacing. These are costs that both buyer and seller must identify and quantify. This concept of value puts price in a clearer perspective. But more to the point, it provides a meaningful rationale for selling and an effective focus for sales attention and effort.

To be more specific, it has been my experience that salespeople are not trained to sell value. They are trained to sell products and to motivate those who buy products. Value is assumed to be intrinsic to what they sell. Hence, the idea is to know the product, its features, its performance; know the competitor's; develop an effective presentation for communicating this information to the customer; and close the sale.

"Closing the sale" assumes that the customer is a specifically identifiable person who has the authority to say yes or no and who buys for emotional and psychological reasons. The customer— that assumed identifiable buyer—is insecure, enjoys power, wants to be mothered, needs stroking. So successful selling is simply a matter of knowing what makes the buyer tick and manipulating his psyche accordingly.

Further, much sales training deals solely with the art and practice of selling as derived from consumer product and service markets. Such training addresses the matters of customer prospecting, getting attention, developing customer interest, making effective presentations, and closing. And indeed every professional salesperson must develop skills in all of these areas. But to be successful, industrial selling must be guided and directed by a clear and viable philosophy.

Products do not sell themselves. And professional buyers are not programmed creatures responding mechanically and uniformly to some psychological stimulus. To begin with, in industrial, commercial, and institutional markets, products and services are not bought for themselves. They are bought to satisfy some need or achieve some result that the buyer's business demands—lower operating costs, improved product quality, increased market share. Also, in these markets the buying process is formalized so that the purchasing decision is not the act of one individual; it's a procedure involving multiple individuals. The "customer," therefore, is in reality a network of buying influences.

Clearly, customer requirements vary, and customer notions of cost vary. Value selling addresses both requirements and costs. Value selling, therefore, is a creative and problem-solving process which provides technical, operational, and economic reasons to persuade customers that the product or service offered satisfies their requirements at the lowest total cost. It is a process which identifies real or potential problems that jeopardize the satisfaction of requirements of the people who influence buying decisions. And it is a process that relates product and service features to those identified buyer requirements and creatively relates those requirements to cost savings or cost avoidance to the customer.

In the following pages, I will develop in detail the principles and techniques of value selling—a strategy for selling in today's cost-conscious markets.

Chapter 1

VALUE AND ITS MEANING TO THE INDUSTRIAL CUSTOMER

The dictionary defines *value* as "an amount considered to be a suitable equivalent for something else . . . a fair price . . . monetary or material worth—worth in usefulness or importance to the possessor—utility or merit. . . ."

Economists define value in more technical terms, but similarly. They identify *value in exchange*, which in layman's terms is simply the price commanded in exchange for goods and services; *value in use*, the function that a product or service performs, which in turn satisfies some user's needs or wants; and *esteem value*, the prestige or psychic gratification associated with a product or a service.

Whether we accept the dictionary's or the economists' definition, what's important is that value resides in the perception of the buyer. It is not intrinsic to the product.

The expression of value to the buyer of a highly standardized product such as a share of stock, a gallon of gasoline, or a pound

1

of salt is likely to be the same as it is for every other buyer of that product. And that is the price that a competitive supply-demand market will allow.

On the other hand, the expression of value for a product that entails special design or manufacture and considerable service and support in its use varies widely from buyer to buyer, depending on factors such as need, specific application, criticalness of use, and unique or special demands of the buyer's products, processes, or markets.

Finally, the expression of value to the buyer of an original Picasso is that highly subjective assessment of the esteem, prestige, or psychological satisfaction it provides.

Perceptions of value are objective when value is seen only in the competitive price—that is, value in exchange—but highly subjective when seen only as a gratification of esteem or psychic urge. However, both objective and subjective considerations are entailed when perceptions of value involve a product's usefulness or utility—that is, value in use. But whether the product bought is a gallon of gasoline or an original Picasso, it does involve cost to the buyer.

Price, the amount of money given for that gasoline or that Picasso, is a cost to the buyer, but not the only one. There are also real costs in using that gasoline in terms of miles per gallon it provides before refueling, or in safeguarding that Picasso, not to mention the opportunity costs of returns on investment lost because the money spent is now tied up in the painting.

To the buyer of the Picasso original, those additional costs may seem unimportant or not deserving of concern because the esteem value in its possession is so great. In the case of the gasoline, the buyer may not even acknowledge or be aware of costs other than the price. In that event, those costs won't enter into the buying decision. But cost to the buyer is a dimension of value, and value selling is a concept of selling that seeks to identify and quantify that dimension to influence the sale.

In the Introduction I defined *value* as "the satisfaction of customer requirements at the lowest total cost in use." That definition is basic to the concept of value selling because it addresses both dimensions of value—customer perceptions of it and costs involved in satisfying those perceptions.

"Customer requirements" may reflect perceptions of value that are those of value in exchange (price), value in use, or esteem value. But in all cases the satisfaction of those "requirements" entails cost.

When value is seen only as value in exchange, price is the only cost the buyer acknowledges. When value is seen only as esteem value, not even price will be given much weight in the buying decision.

But industrial sales situations involving pure considerations of esteem value are few and far between. More typically, the salesperson is dealing with buyer perceptions of value involving various considerations of value in use and value in exchange. Both of these reflect the common denominator of dollars and cents of cost—first cost, that is, price of the product or service, and subsequent cost, the cost in use.

Buyers in industrial, commercial, and institutional markets buy primarily for use value. Unlike the consumer buyer, they do not buy to satisfy a personal need or want. They buy to satisfy some requirement of their business, their product or processes, or their very purpose for being. They buy to supply or service customers or clients, to manufacture product, to maintain plant or equipment. And they buy to improve quality, to meet competition, to operate efficiently within constraints of technology, time, and cost.

These are all external factors impinging on the buyer, so industrial demand is a derived demand. It is a demand derived from these external factors. And as such, the prime objective in buying to satisfy that demand is to acquire the perceived values in use at the lowest possible cost.

Value Analysis

An activity performed in most large corporations, as well as in many government agencies, is known as *value analysis*. Value analysis is an organized approach to achieve the lowest cost at which a particular product, material, or service performs its necessary or intended function. A function is any feature, characteristic, or element of performance that makes a product work or sell.

Functions are best defined by using a verb-noun combination. For example, the function of treads on an automobile tire is to *provide traction;* the function of a rubber washer around the faucet assembly is to *prevent leaking.*

Functions are *basic* and *secondary.* Basic functions are those that are necessary for the effective and reliable working of the product. They make a product do what it is intended to do. Functions are secondary when they are not critical to the product's use but satisfy aesthetic considerations or enhance the product's individuality in a competitive market.

A basic function of the television chassis, for example, is to *contain the tube and inner workings* of the instrument. And that will dictate elements of design, configuration, and materials if that chassis is to contain them effectively. Considerations of color and finish of the chassis are secondary functions and contribute only to the instrument's appearance. Value analysis systematically reviews the functions—primary and secondary—and the costs of supplying them in a product, component, material, or service in order to achieve the lowest cost in acquiring those functions.

The formal application of value analysis in industry goes back to 1947. It is generally acknowledged that it started with the General Electric Company and that Larry Miles, a GE staff engineer, was the prime mover in its development and acceptance.

Because purchased materials and services represented the largest single element of product cost, value analysis was initially applied to purchased items. It was then applied to items manufactured internally and subsequently to the original product design process. At this point, the activity became known as *value engineering,* and that term seems to have supplanted the original one.

Regardless of what it is called, value analysis-value engineering is a structured discipline that seeks answers to five key questions:

1. What is the item, the product material or service?
2. What does it do, and what functions does it perform?
3. What does it cost, and what do the functions cost?
4. What else could do what needs to be done, or provide the functions required?
5. What would that cost?

And in making buying decisions, organizations that employ value analysis-value engineering measure value by ten tests:

1. Does the item's use contribute value?
2. Is its cost proportionate to its usefulness?
3. Does it need all of its features?
4. Is there anything better for the intended use?
5. Can an equally usable item be made by a lower-cost method?
6. Can a standard product be found which will be usable?
7. Is it made on proper tooling, considering quantities used?
8. Do material, reasonable labor, overhead, and profit add up to total cost?
9. Will another dependable supplier provide it for less?
10. Is anyone buying it for less?

Whether or not value analysis-value engineering is a formal and organized activity, the principles of the discipline are widely known and practiced in industry today. They originated to stem the escalating costs of production in the post-World War II environment of scarcity and shortage. They were reinforced and more extensively applied in subsequent years. More recently, the combined effects of foreign competition, hyper-inflation, high cost of capital, and the most serious recession since the 1930s made value analysis-value engineering a matter of industrial survival in the 1980s. And that is a fact those who sell to industry must understand.

The industrial, commercial, or institutional buyer's perception of value is first and foremost value in use. The buyer is concerned with what the product or service does, how it functions, and what utility or usefulness it provides. But the buyer is also concerned with its cost and seeks the lowest cost at which that utility can be obtained. If there is no obvious difference in usefulness in what is offered by one seller versus another, and no costs other than price are acknowledged, the buyer will choose the product or service with the lowest price.

In industrial and institutional markets, the customer does not buy to satisfy personal wants or desires but to satisfy requirements of the business or to meet product or process demands. Further, the customer is rarely a single individual making buying decisions alone. The "customer" is an organization of different individuals, each having different functional responsibilities in buying within structured and formalized procedures. The larger the organization, the more structured and formalized those buying procedures are.

As the largest of all institutional buyers, the federal government and its myriad agencies epitomize structured and formalized buying. All authority to buy derives from the laws that establish the agency or provide the authorization for some legislative program or purpose. The authority to buy is vested in the head of the agency, who in turn delegates it to a procurement office. Government officers and employees who are authorized to function as procurement and contracting officers must act in accordance with the applicable law, and within the prescribed constraints of their delegated authority. This fact has significant implications for those who sell to the government "customer" and is discussed in Chapter 7 in more detail.

Similarly, all publicly owned industrial customers buy under formalized authorization. The authority to buy is derived from the corporate charter and is vested through the board of directors and a presiding chief executive officer. In turn this authority is delegated and vested invariably in a purchasing office.

If a company is decentralized, with operating autonomy at division or plant levels, the authority to buy will be decentralized also. In some cases there will be a purchasing authorization at both the corporate and division-plant levels. This split may be in terms of commodity, so that products having common application in multiple division-plant locations may be bought centrally out of the corporate office. Materials and services that are unique to a division-plant location may be bought locally. In either event, it is clear that the authority to commit the industrial corporate customer legally and procedurally resides in the purchasing office.

But whether it be government or industrial buying, the process of procurement is a multistep and multifunctional one. A need—technically called a requirement—must be identified and authorized. Requirements may originate anywhere within the organization, but authorization for outside purchases can be made only if the necessary funds are available. These funds are in an operating unit's budget, or they are specifically made available by higher management out of other budget sources.

By far, the major purchase requirements of the industrial customer are for materials, components, supplies, and services associated with what it sells. The major requirements of the institutional customer are for those same factors, but as they are employed in military and defense, health and welfare, transportation, environmental, or other areas of institutional mandate. Fully fifty cents of the industrial customer's sales dollar goes out through purchase of these factors from outside suppliers. In the case of the military, 60 to 75 percent of its budget is for systems, supplies, and services from outside contractors.

If funds are available through the budget or provided through special appropriation, a requirement must then be adequately described for purchase. Its description may take the form of a government, commercial, or professional society "specification." Federal government specifications, for example, are intended spe cifically for government use. In some cases they cover materials to be used, methods of manufacture, tolerances, dimensions, color, and type of finish. In other cases, such specifications cover supplies, equipment, and services normally produced for sale to the general public and available from commercial sources. Specifications covering products and services for sale to the public relate primarily to the use, operation, or performance of the item rather than to details of its construction or considerations deemed unimportant or superficial. The typical industrial customer will specify requirements in similar fashion.

If the requirement is for a material or component that will become part of what the company makes and sells, specifying it is done in an engineering activity. The individual responsible for this function carries the title of design engineer, component engineer, or material engineer, and the activity is generally known as Product or Design Engineering. A requirement for an item of equipment or a service related to the plant, facility, or processes employed in manufacture or operation is specified by an engineer in some Plant Engineering, Facility, or Process Engineering activity. If the requirement is for data processing equipment or services, the specifying is done by some systems or management specialist in Management Information Systems, Finance, or the Controller's office.

Generally speaking, requirements are specified by those technically qualified to do so. The more complex or advanced the technology involved, the more technically trained and experienced will be the specifier. Simpler, routine requirements are more often specified by operational, nonengineering types.

The industrial-institutional customer describes requirements not only by technical specifications but also in terms of quantity and time. In the case of production materials, quantity and time specifications are dictated by two considerations:

1. The demands of the customer's market, which in turn determine manufacturing and distribution plans and schedules; plant operating rates; and machine and manpower utilization
2. The establishment, maintenance, and replenishment of inventories to support these

Quantity and time requirements for every item going into the customer's product are determined by planners and schedulers found in Production or Inventory Control, Materials Management, or in some cases in Purchasing itself.

Where planning and scheduling activities are computerized, quantity and time requirements are determined electronically. In most large industrial companies, this phase of the procurement process is accomplished through computerized Materials Requirements Planning (MRP).

MRP uses bills of materials, inventory and open order data, and master scheduling information to calculate quantity and time requirements for all materials going into products produced. It is time-phased, so all changes in market demand are reflected automatically in rescheduled quantities and due dates on all open orders. Computerized MRP is steadily reducing the role of personal planners and schedulers in determining quantity and time requirements.

Once requirements are defined by technical specifications and in terms of quantity and time, the specifying or using activity initiates a written requisition, the formal authorization allowing

Purchasing to buy. It contains all the requirements and the budget line item or account number against which the expenditure will be charged. It may also include a recommended source or sources, and it is on this point that purchasing offices, industrial as well as government, have exerted growing influence.

The position they take is that the task of defining or describing the requirement is the function of the specifier or user. The task of selecting the source is Purchasing's. Hence, in most of the larger industrial organizations, a requisition that identifies or recommends a source must also acknowledge an "or equal." This means that Purchasing can seek out a source other than the recommended one and buy from that source if it is in fact "equal."

The extent to which this actually occurs obviously varies from company to company. But the point is that selection of supplier and negotiation of supplier agreements are responsibilities jealously defended in most purchasing organizations. Further, in most large companies this discretion is also formally recognized by higher management in the Purchasing charters or policy guides they approve and publish.

Although the legal commitment to buy may reside in Purchasing, it is clear that the buyer or purchasing agent is not the "customer." The customer is the total company or institution that specifies, uses, evaluates, and maintains as well as places the order for what is bought. And these activities are performed by different individuals who have different functional interests and objectives. Unlike the consumer-buyer, who embodies all of these activities himself, the industrial-institutional customer is multifunctioned and multileveled. The consumer-buyer expresses his motive to buy—emotional or otherwise—in a personal decision; the industrial-institutional customer goes through a complex process of analyzing, compromising, and formalizing before that buying decision can be made.

To put it simply: In industrial-institutional markets, the customer is the sum total of buying influences. Those influences reside in those who

- Budget, approve, or appropriate the funds necessary to make the purchase

- Specify, describe, or define requirements in the technical terms of design, performance, reliability, materials, components, trade name identification, and testing and inspection criteria
- Specify quantities, delivery and completion dates, transportation and handling conditions, and other nontechnical service support
- Use, operate, and maintain what is bought so that from experience they can access and evaluate past and current supplier performance

Finally, there is the visible buying influence of the buyer or purchasing agent, who processes the requisition; invites quotations, competitive or not; places the purchase order; approves the invoice; and ensures completion or compliance with the order so that payment can be made. The buyer's visibility as the "customer" is obvious, because without issuance of the purchase order or approvals for payment, no payment will be forthcoming. The significance and extent of the buyer or purchasing agent's actual buying influence, however, is another matter.

The more standardized or commercially available the requirement, and the more repetitive its purchase, the stronger will be the buying influence of Purchasing. The more technically unusual or complex the requirement and the more it reflects a one-time or infrequent purchase, the stronger will be the buying influence of specifiers or users.

Buying influences, however, are rarely fixed and constant. They vary with time, personalities involved, economic conditions, organizational changes, and other factors. But for anyone to sell successfully to the industrial-institutional customer, the buying influences must be correctly identified and assessed.

Further, since Purchasing personnel and specifiers have different functional interests and objectives, salespeople must learn not only to assess the buying influence of each but also to communicate with them in the one common language they all understand: the dollars and cents of the cost involved in satisfying requirements.

Value selling is cost-justifying selling. It identifies and quantifies to personnel with buying influence how a sale

- Reduces cost
- Avoids cost
- Offsets cost through increased income or improved cash flow

Its aim is to satisfy requirements at the least cost to the customer.

Chapter 2

BUYING INFLUENCES AND THEIR VALUE PERCEPTIONS

According to a recent report, the average cost of calling on an industrial customer in 1988 was $217.92. That was an increase of 22 percent over the 1986 cost of $178.96.* Additionally, many more face-to-face presentations are required before making a sale than ever before.

Two conclusions can be drawn from the data:

1. The industrial customer has become more difficult to sell.
2. The effectiveness of industrial selling is declining.

---

* "1989 Survey of Selling Costs," *Sales & Marketing Management*, Vol. 141, No. 3 (February 20, 1989), p. 15.

The fact is that both conclusions may be valid, because they both reflect a single, common development. Industrial customers have changed in their buying attitudes and practices. But industrial selling has not fully recognized or adjusted to that change. Hence, more calls per sale are required to find the right person for telling the sales story to and to develop the right sales story for the right person.

Now, what are the changes that have taken place in industrial markets and how have they affected industrial sales? There are two major changes, and together they have made the task of industrial selling significantly more complex.

First, there is the increased formalization of the procurement process with its policies and practices more heavily influenced by financial and accounting considerations. Whereas the industrial salesman once sold on the basis of friendship, or to acknowledged decision makers in Engineering, Production, or elsewhere, there are now formal purchasing procedures that must be followed. The customers spell out days and times for his visits, people to call on, how quotations and proposals are to be made, how they will be evaluated, and so forth. Purchasing has become the clearing house for sales submissions, and the purchasing agent or buyer is a prime point of customer contact.

The second major change is the growing volatility of industrial demand. Value perceptions are constantly shifting because of altered technical, financial, and other priorities. Where technical excellence may be weighted heavily in buying decisions one day, it is less important than price advantage the next. And this shifting perception of value is not always clear or predictable. It is the complex result of exploding technology, broadening markets and competition, the high cost of capital, and the chronic uncertainties of modern economics and society. Its immediate consequence, however, is that not only are the people who influence buying decisions changing, but their sense of priorities is changing as well.

It was mentioned in Chapter 1 that in industrial markets the "customer" is the sum total of buying influences. *Buying influences* are "all those individuals who can say yes or no to a product or service." Thus, the key question to ask when selling to these markets is: "Which of the many people who perform different functions or exercise different responsibilities at different levels within the organization can say yes or no, and for what reasons?"

In view of the two major changes in industrial markets—increased formalization of the procurement process and increased volatility of industrial demand—it is clear that the number of buying influences the salesperson must recognize has increased. Although there may be only one major influence who can say yes, there are more and more who can say no. And this complicates the problem of selling, because the major influence who can say yes may never have the opportunity of doing so if some meaningful influence has said no somewhere else in the buying process.

Further, given the shifting priorities in value perceptions of buying influences, the major influence who said yes before may say no now. And he may do so for reasons he does not understand or agree with. Nonetheless, lacking the authority or the ammunition to act counter to the prevailing priority in his company's value perceptions, he says no. So again, the critical question in industrial selling is "Who can say yes or no, and for what reasons?"

It should be obvious that there is no precise answer to this question for all customers in all industrial markets. But there is a rationale that the salesperson can follow in identifying buying influences and their strengths in specific selling situations. There are also rationales for learning and handling shifting value perceptions, so that one can address and deal more effectively with those reasons for saying no. Let's explore those rationales.

Market Categories

Industrial demand is derived demand. It is derived from the demands of the customer's markets, products, and processes. Hence, we can look to the nature and content of those derived demands to gain some insights into the industrial customer's value perceptions and the key buying influences likely to reflect them. For example, the nature and content of the customer's markets are prime determinants of why and how he buys. Industrial markets can be broken down into the following three categories.

In each category the nature of the market differs, so customer motivations to buy differ as well.

1. *End-user markets*—those in which customers buy to consume or use products and services within their own manufacturing or operational processes. They buy for the function or the utility of the product or service to those processes. They buy to maintain, repair, or operate facilities and equipment. They buy to service or support plant and people.
2. *Resale markets*—those in which customers buy to resell at a profit. Customers include wholesalers, distributors, jobbers, and others who buy to hold or move products directly to their customers at some markup from cost.
3. *Original equipment manufacturers* (OEMs)—customers who buy to incorporate what they buy into their own product or service offerings, either in some altered state or as is. Prime considerations in their buying are the integrity of their product's design, performance, and reliability as well as its competitiveness in their marketplace.

A fourth market is that of the *combination customer,* who buys a product for more than one purpose. An industrial customer, for example, may buy a valve or bearing in all three capacities. He may incorporate these products as components in the product he manufactures as an OEM. He may resell these products as replacements to his customers as a reseller. And he may also consume these products in the maintenance or repair of his manufacturing equipment as an end user. Because he buys for various purposes, the combination buyer does not usually have a common motivation toward that buying. Further, because of antitrust laws, he may be constrained from buying them, and have to resort to a common strategy. Hence, combination buying does not warrant a special category for our analysis purposes.

Product/Service Categories

As the nature and content of the customer's markets determine *why* he buys, the demands of his products and processes determine *what* he buys. What the industrial customer buys runs the gamut from nuts and bolts and cotter pins to turbines, radioactive materials, and highly specialized technical services. But for our purposes everything he buys may be seen as falling into one of the following classifications. Depending on which classification a purchase falls into, value perceptions and buying influences that apply will be affected differently.

Commodities—Uniform, homogeneous products that are sold in broad commercial markets. They are products that typically manifest four characteristics:

1. They are produced to common standards and specifications.
2. They are sold for general purpose or application.
3. They are produced in anticipation of market demand.
4. They are sold from existing stocks.

Commodities are basics like copper, steel, cotton, or corn. They are also end products like capacitors, semiconductors, motors, and switches that are sold commercially in general markets. If markets see no distinction in the offerings of their commodity suppliers, competitive price will be the prime factor in their source selection.

Specialty products—Products produced to some special design, specification, performance, or application. They may involve a modification of a standard product, in which event a significant factor in the customer's attitude will be the extent of the modification. If the modification is slight, the product will resemble a commodity and the customer will view it accordingly; if it is major, the product will be considered a true special. Or, the product may be of unique design and meet unique performance and environmental criteria. The more specialized the product, the more apt it is to be bought with price considerations secondary to technical ones. However, many salespeople delude themselves by believing that their offerings are unique, while their customers view them simply as commodities.

Services—Personal time expended in such areas as engineering, construction, maintenance, repair, finance, data processing, advertising, consulting, and law. Services include intangibles like insurance, health care, or pension fund management. Services may be routine or highly specialized. Unlike commodities and specialty products, however, they cannot be inventoried. Services cannot be put on a shelf and stored. Further, when services are needed, they are usually needed immediately. This means that services are less subject to the accounting and financial controls which are the rule with products that become part of the customer's inventories. And because they involve personal effort or performance, services are less subject to competitive comparison than products.

Systems—Combinations of products and services that satisfy multiple needs of the customer through engineering, management, and other support. Unlike a simple package of products, whose benefit to the customer is merely the sum of the individual products themselves, a system is synergistic. Through its design or service support, it fills particular needs in a unique way. The growing concern of industrial customers with the improvement of quality through process controls and with the improvement of inventory through production controls is leading to an increasing demand for systems of all kinds. Systems are rarely bought by one individual. Their purchase is typically the result of some team effort.

In summary, therefore, we have three distinct kinds of industrial customers, the nature and content of whose markets determine *why* they buy. Additionally, we have four distinct kinds of market offerings that can satisfy customer product and process needs. These determine *what* they buy.

The industrial salesperson must ask these questions:

- Into what market category does my customer or prospective customer fall? Is he a user or reseller of what I sell or is he an OEM?
- Into what category does my market offering fall? Is it a commodity or specialty product? Is it a service or a system combining product and service? Most important, how does the customer view my offering?

The "customer's view" of an offering is that reflected in the value perceptions of buying influences. Hence, the next question to pursue is, "Who are those buying influences?"

Buying Influences

One buying influence always present is Purchasing. And the increased formalization of the procurement process alluded to in the beginning of this chapter has increased Purchasing's involvement in the buying decision. Regardless of the type of industry or size of the company involved, invariably we find a purchasing activity formally in place within the organizational structure. In large companies like IBM, General Electric, or General Motors, that function may include thousands of buyers, purchasing managers, and materials managers. In an increasing number of cases, the function is headed up by a corporate vice-president or director reporting at the highest levels of corporate management.

The authority of Purchasing is spelled out in corporate charters, corporate policy statements, manuals, and directives, whose language is all fairly typical:

> It will be the responsibility of the Purchasing Department to conduct negotiations and make all final commitments for materials, supplies, and services as required. . . .

> The charter of Purchasing is to improve business results by supplying company operations with raw materials, equipment, supplies, and services at optimum cost and service levels. . . .

> Purchasing will negotiate for and make commitments on all commodities, supplies, equipment, and services at optimal cost, in accordance with quality, quantity, and time requirements. . . .

Purchasing Authority

The exercise of purchasing responsibility or authority in most large companies will vary depending on the nature and mix of their business. For example, the more diversified the company's mix of products and processes, the more apt it is to have decentralized purchasing activities. At each product division or manufacturing operation, there will be an autonomous purchasing department that buys the materials, supplies, and services used at that level or location. There may or may not be a corporate purchasing office. If there is, it will have direct buying authority only over those materials and services that are used in common at multiple divisions and operations. And even for these, the corporate office may negotiate only pricing and supply agreements with selected suppliers, leaving the actual commitments for specific quantities and deliveries to the decentralized units. In some cases, the corporate purchasing office may do no actual buying at all. It may merely set policies, provide guidance and direction to Purchasing at the decentralized operations, and exercise functional planning, reporting, and liaison at the corporate level.

In industries with limited products or services, for example, petroleum, bulk chemicals, food processing, gas and electric utilities, and transportation, the purchasing function tends to be more centralized. Buying authority is heavily concentrated in a corporate purchasing office, particularly over those raw materials, equipment, and services that make up a major share of product or service cost.

Whether it be a decentralized or single-product or single-service industry, however, Purchasing is definitely a buying influence in all industrial markets. And industrial salespeople must recognize that fact. Even if Purchasing cannot give the ultimate "yes," it can interject the equivocal "yes, but. . . ." And this can often kill a sale as effectively as an unequivocal "no."

The actual strength of Purchasing's buying influence in any specific instance is determined by many factors. Some of these are difficult to generalize about, so salespeople must assess them on a case-by-case basis. For example:

- What is the experience or technical or business background of the buyer, how much initiative and assertiveness does he have, and how does his ability to see the bigger picture compare with his concern for procedure or detail?
- How is the buyer or the purchasing department seen by other functions? Is Purchasing recognized and respected as technically capable of making source and value judgments? Or are they viewed primarily as order placers?
- Are there written policies and procedures, and are they adhered to in regard to non-Purchasing contacts with suppliers, sub-

mission of samples, bidding procedures, authority to make changes, and personal liability for making commitments outside of authorized capacity?

- Does Purchasing have the visible and active support of higher management to fulfill its responsibilities as its charter or statement of objectives defines them?

The successful industrial salesperson knows the answers to these questions. Those who aspire to success must make it their business to learn them.

However, all salespeople can improve their sales effectiveness by better assessing the buying influence of Purchasing compared with that of others within the customer structure. These "others" are those whose judgment or opinion tends to be reflected in the customer's buying decisions. Their opinions vary in importance and authority depending on:

- *Why the customer buys.* Is he an end user, a reseller, an OEM?
- *What the customer buys.* Does he buy commodities, special products, services, or systems?

These "other" buying influences can be identified as follows:

Specifiers—Individuals who define purchase requirements in terms of material descriptions, properties, characteristics, or performance. They define them in terms of drawings, specifications, or design criteria. They may also define them by way of trade name or government or professional society standards. Specifiers are technically knowledgeable and experienced enough to decide what is required. In OEMs they are in some engineering capacity. If requirements to be defined are for products, the specifiers will be found in Product or Design Engineering. If requirements are associated with processes, they will be found in Production, Process, or Plant Engineering. Specifiers in some instances may be found in Marketing (for resale items), Financial Management (for data processing equipment and services), and in other activities for specialized needs.

Users—Those who convert, process, consume, use, maintain, or replace what is bought. All major purchases of production materials and capital equipment are typically charged against the cost of product or against a department's (user's) operating budget. Hence, the user's buying influence is a reflection of his financial or cost accountability for what is bought. Users may also be specifiers. This is often the case with manufacturing, engineering, and office supply items because in most instances such items individually represent small dollar expenditures. As such they do not receive the same financial and accounting control as product materials and capital equipment. Thus, there is less pressure to provide checks and balances between the specifying and the using activities.

Higher management—Customer executives who manage corporate, divisional, or operational units as well as those who manage functional staff activities. They rarely specify or use what is purchased, but they can influence source selection for marketing, public relations, or business strategy reasons.

Figures 2–1 and 2–2 identify the buying influences of functions and people within the customer organization. Figure 2–1 shows that influence in terms of *why* the customer buys: Is he an end user, a reseller, or an OEM? Figure 2–2 shows that influence in terms of *what* he buys: Does he buy commodities, special products, services, or systems? Because the figures deal with factors that are closely interrelated, the grids shown will overlap.

From Figures 2–1 and 2–2, we can summarize the relative strength of buying influences as follows:

Purchasing—A buying influence if for no other reason than it is the authorized agency for committing the customer. Purchasing's real influence, however, will vary. The larger the organization and the more formalized the purchasing process, the stronger will be its influence. That influence will also be strong in the buying of product and process materials, as is always the case in OEM businesses. It is moderate to strong in the purchase of maintenance, repair, and operating supplies in resale and end-user markets. It is weaker in the purchase of capital equipment, specialized services, and systems in all markets. The growing professionalization of Purchasing is a force making for its growing buying influence. Through its application of value analysis-value engineering, vendor rating, and price-cost analysis, Purchasing is making that influence felt in all markets and for all requirements. Purchasing's increased influence is discussed in greater detail in Chapter 8.

(text continues on page 26)

Figure 2-1. Buying influence by type of buyer.

Buying Influence	End User	Reseller	Original Equipment Manufacturer (OEM)
Purchasing	Strong influence if requirement is standard or of low dollar value, as for maintenance, repair, and operating supplies. The larger the organization and the more formalized the buying process, the stronger the influence. Influence is strong over the question of "from whom to buy," weak over the question of "what to buy." Prime examples of end-user Purchasing influence where buying processes are formalized and where buying decisions subject to public scrutiny are in government, utility, and transportation procurement.	Influence is moderate to strong in the purchase of supply items—maintenance, repair, operating, and office supplies. Not as strong in areas of products, materials, and services bought for resale. Buying processes tend to be less formal and structured, so in smaller companies Purchasing may merely process purchase orders, rather than initiate basic purchase decisions.	Strong influence over the purchase of all product and process materials, parts, and components. Influence is weaker in the purchase of capital equipment and professional services. Purchasing has strong influence over source selection and through increasing experience and training of personnel is gaining growing influence over matters of specifications, or what to buy. Influence is small in areas of specialized services, such as legal, advertising, health care, insurance, etc. As a generalization, the larger the company, the stronger the purchasing influence.
Specifiers	Strong influence over determination of what to buy—capable of influencing the decision of from whom to buy by specifying around a particular supplier's offering.	Specifiers and users are often the same person or engaged in the same function. If so, buying influence is strong.	Moderate to strong over products that are vendor designed or proprietary. Influence is weaker over materials, parts, and components that are standardized or commercially available.

Users	Influence is strong over specialized or high-cost capital equipment and professional services. In large organizations that influence is tempered by more formalized buying procedures and by multifunctional buying decisions. Influence is weak over standard, commercially sold, or low-cost supply items.	Major "users" in reseller organizations are those who market what is bought, and their buying influence is strong not only over "what to buy," but also over "from whom to buy." Users of maintenance, repair, operating, and office supplies have only moderate buying influence.	Influence is moderate to strong over specialized process equipment, instrumentation, test equipment, and related professional services. Influence is weak over maintenance, repair, operating, and office supplies and services. Buying influence is comparatively stronger in smaller OEMs than in larger, more formally organized ones.
Higher Management	Does not usually become involved in buying decisions except for major requirements, such as data processing systems, insurance, health care benefits, pension and financial programs, and specialized services. Influence is more in areas of source selection than in those of specifying and may reflect considerations of marketing or community relations.	Strong influence over the selection of sources for major products or materials for resale. Strong also over the selection of sources for marketing-related services, such as transportation, distribution, and advertising and promotion. Does not usually become involved in purchase of maintenance, repair, and operating supplies.	The larger the company, the less involved higher management will be in buying decisions—influence is negligible over most product materials. Influence will be stronger over specialized services, such as legal, financial, and advertising. For important marketing or other considerations, higher management may influence source selection involving large dollar purchases.

Figure 2-2. Buying influence over what is bought.

Buying Influence	Commodities	Special Products	Services	Systems
Purchasing	Strong influence, particularly over low-cost items. Influence is stronger in large OEM businesses where product and process materials are involved. Influence is weaker in reseller business.	Moderate to strong over products or process items. Less strong where special products are for end-use consumption. Negligible influence when bought for resale.	Moderate to strong over manufacturing services, such as machining and assembly, as well as repair and maintenance services. Less influence over specialized or professional services. In large, formally structured organizations, Purchasing influence is always exercised over pricing and contract negotiations to some degree.	Influence is less, because systems are typically bought by teams of multifunctional people. Purchasing may act as team leader in larger organizations, and its influence will reflect solely the skill and experience of the Purchasing representative rather than the importance of the function to the buying decision.
Specifiers	Influence is negligible—by definition commodities are standard and commercially available. Once specified as such, their source selection is largely a competitive price consideration.	Influence is significant because specifier may specify requirements around a particular supplier's unique product design or features. By so doing, the specifier strongly influences source selection.	Influence is moderate to strong in the case of professional or specialized services for the same reasons as for special products. Influence is less on routine manufacturing, repair, and operating services.	Influence is moderate to the extent that system requirements can be specified around a particular supplier's design and performance capabilities.

Users	Influence is negligible. Exceptions occur when commodities have trade names and users are comfortable with their use. If they are low-cost items, their purchase will not be challenged by Purchasing.	Influence can be significant where users are also specifiers. Influence is only moderate where specifying and using activities are separate and buying process is formalized.	Influence is moderate to strong over professional and specialized services. Moderate to weak over routine manufacturing, repair, and operating services.	Moderate to strong influence in their ability to influence performance requirements of systems. Influence is less over selection of system's source due to multifunctional nature of systems buying.
Higher Management	Influence is negligible except where commodities are a major element of product or process cost. Such is the case in the commodity resale business (steel warehousing) and in basic process industries, such as chemical, petroleum, and food processing.	Higher management does not usually become involved in buying decisions except where special products entail a major element of product or process costs, as is the case with commodities.	Influence is moderate to strong over professional and specialized services that are companywide in their impact, such as financial, legal, advertising, and insurance services. Does not usually get involved in buying decisions over routine operating services.	Influence is strongest in small- to medium-size organizations. In larger organizations, influence is less because of the multifunctional nature of systems buying and the structured, formalized buying process of larger organizations.

Specifiers—A buying influence, by definition. They define and describe what is to be purchased. To the extent that their specifications are in terms of materials, designs, properties, or performance features that can be satisfied by multiple suppliers, their real buying influence is limited. Any experienced purchasing agent or buyer will invariably put that specification out for competitive bidding and select a source by that process. To the extent that the specifier can define or describe the requirement in terms of a particular supplier's unique design or performance characteristics, however, his real buying influence is significant. In specifying as he does, he tends to preselect the source.

Users—A buying influence because the purchase is often charged against their product or operating budgets. Since they have cost accountability for what is bought, they exert some influence over the buying decision. That influence, however, varies because of several factors. In large, formally structured organizations, there is a separation of function and authority over questions of using and buying for use. Hence, users have less buying influence in larger organizations than in smaller ones, except where major or one-time expenditures are involved. Again in larger organizations, there is usually a separation of the specifying and using activities. In smaller ones, the specifier and user may be the same person, so his buying influence is greater. The buying influence of users in all organizations is stronger over specialized equipment, instrumentation, and services than it is over standard products or routine services.

Higher management—Less of a buying influence than is generally assumed. This is particularly true in large, formally structured organizations, where a separation of responsibility and authority is made in the activities of specifying, using, and buying. Higher management in all types of business rarely becomes involved in the day-to-day buying decisions for product and process materials and services. It may, however, get involved in major procurements that impact strongly on product or process costs. This is certainly the case in the purchase of major items for resale, or in the purchase of critical and costly product or process equipment. Higher management is usually involved in the purchase of specialized functions like legal, advertising, and financial services and, accordingly, is a strong buying influence in those areas.

Chapter 3

THE MEANING OF
COST AND THE
RELATIONSHIP OF
COST TO VALUE

Value perceptions necessarily reflect the functional interests and objectives of buying influences. To illustrate:

• Value to a *design engineer* is the assurance of performance or reliability in what he specifies. That assurance may be satisfied by a particular supplier's proprietary item, or it may be satisfied by the engineer's own design, material, or performance specifications. In any event, value is a technical consideration. It is that which satisfies the engineer's sense of design integrity, for which he is functionally responsible.

• Value to the *purchasing agent* may be seen simply in terms of price. If specifications are clear and sources are approved and readily available, the competitive price is a reasonable expression of value to him. Whether he buys for a large or small company, the purchasing agent is evaluated in terms of prices paid. Hence, his notions of value are largely price-related.

• Value to the *production manager* is guaranteed availability of materials and supplies to keep machines and manpower running. It is the ensured capability of meeting production schedules on time and at planned levels of capacity and is largely a consideration of logistics. Hence, value is assumed in a seller's perceived capability to supply specified quantities at specified times.

And so it goes with all buying influences. Their perceptions of value are related to their functional responsibilities. How and for what they are held accountable determines their view of value. And with business and functional activities becoming more specialized, value perceptions can easily become narrow and restricted. Worse, they may compete and conflict with one another.

But there is one common factor that transcends all functional considerations: the common factor of cost. *Cost* is the yardstick of all business measurement. Together with income, it is the basis of profit and loss determination. Uncontrolled cost can jeopardize the very survival of a business or institution.

Every purchase entails cost, so every buying decision has cost consequences. When a buying influence makes a judgment as to specification or source, a stream of future costs is set in motion. These costs include not only the cost implicit in the price but also those that extend through receipt, handling, use, replacement, or sale. From their narrow functional perspectives, buying influences may be conscious of only one area where cost is affected. To the extent they ignore other areas, however, they sacrifice value.

In order for salespeople to be effective value sellers, therefore, they must understand customer costs not only as they are accounted for but also in terms of their relationships to function, to customer objectives, and to value contribution. The value seller must understand what costs are affected by the purchase decision and learn to present his offering in terms of total cost-effectiveness.

The Accounting View of Cost

Accounting systems differentiate between direct and overhead costs.

Direct costs are those so clearly or closely related to the production of the customer's product or service that they can be calculated easily. You can determine how much direct cost goes into a single unit of a product or service. For example, if the customer assembles purchased components into a finished product, the cost of that assembly labor and the cost of those purchased components are direct costs because the purchased items become an integral part of the product itself. The parts are then assembled by labor, which configures and combines them to the product's specified design.

In most manufacturing and distribution businesses, as well as in services like building construction, direct costs are the major costs of doing business. Direct material costs, for example, may make up thirty to seventy-five cents of the net sales dollar. Therefore, those who sell direct materials to industry must appreciate the impact of what they sell on the customer's costs and profitability.

Indirect costs, also known as *overhead costs,* do not result from the production of a specific unit or quantity of product or service. Supervision, inspection, rent, depreciation, operating supplies, and administrative expenses are all overhead costs. They are costs associated with the overall conduct of the customer's business, and are not a direct result of what he produces and sells. As a consequence, overhead costs cannot be easily charged directly to the product or service as actually incurred. Rather, they are allocated or apportioned to them by some method of approximation. In capital-intensive industries like petroleum refining, drug and pharmaceutical manufacturing, and transportation and electric utilities, overhead costs make up a major portion of total cost.

The significance of distinguishing between direct and indirect costs for the value seller lies in the fact that they are perceived differently within the customer organization. Direct costs of purchased materials or services, for example, are captured and charged directly against the product, the order, or the contract for which they are bought. Whether they are charged as actually incurred or at some predetermined standard cost, they have strong visibility. If they are higher than what was estimated or allowed for in the price at which the customer sells, their impact is negative and direct on profit and loss. If they are lower, their impact is positive and again direct on profit and loss. Hence, direct material costs are perceived in their profit-loss relationship.

What the customer's accounting system identifies as "direct material cost" is largely determined by the price of those materials. Even if the customer employs a standard cost-accounting system, the direct material cost standard will reflect past or projected purchase prices. Accordingly, salespeople should recognize that perceptions of value for direct materials can easily be confined to considerations of price alone.

Further, because of the direct relationship between purchase price paid and profit and loss, that value perception of direct materials can be firmly entrenched among buying influences held directly accountable for profit and loss. Among these are purchasing and production managers in manufacturing industries, product or marketing managers in resale or distribution businesses, and project managers in construction and other service industries. Because of their background and orientation, financial managers also tend to perceive value primarily in terms of purchase price.

The implications of this limited value perception are important to those who sell. If it goes unchallenged and uncorrected, the buying decision will be based on the lowest price available. Competition will be seen simply as price versus price. Value selling addresses the need to challenge and correct that limited perception. We shall demonstrate how in the following pages.

Although accounting systems may not classify them as such, costs are also distinguishable as variable or fixed. *Variable costs* are those the customer incurs specifically because he produces a given product or service he sells. These costs vary directly with production volume or activity. They represent actual cash that the customer pays out when he produces or performs but retains when he does not. It doesn't matter whether that cash is paid out immediately or at some time in the future.

Variable costs include such things as the amount of inventory the customer employs or the amount of material he buys to produce a product or perform a service he sells. For example, if every time he grinds a part going into his product he uses eight cents' worth of machining fluid and one abrasive disk worth seventeen cents, the variable cost for this one operation will be twenty-five cents. If the customer grinds 100 parts in a day, his variable cost will be $25. If he grinds no parts, his variable cost for this operation will be zero.

Fixed costs, on the other hand, are costs the customer incurs simply by virtue of being in business; they are the same no matter what the production volume may be. For example, the depreciation cost on the grinding machine used in the operation just discussed may be $75 per month. If the customer grinds 100 units per day for the entire month, his monthly depreciation cost will be $75. If he produces nothing and the grinding machine lies idle, he will still have a monthly depreciation cost of $75. Fixed costs, therefore, represent:

• Money that the customer has already put into buildings or equipment and that he cannot get back
• Money that he will have to pay out in the future whether he performs production work or leaves his facilities idle

Examples of fixed costs other than depreciation are rent, property taxes, interest on borrowed capital, executive salaries, and general office and administrative expenses.

There is a hybrid category of costs known as *semivariable,* which are partially variable and partially fixed. For example, the depreciation on a customer's warehouse is a fixed cost. During certain times of the year, he may rent additional space to meet seasonal demand requirements. If depreciation is $1,000 a month and his rent for additional space is $300 a month, his semivariable cost for the months he rents is $1,000 fixed plus $300 variable, or $1,300.

All direct costs are 100 percent variable costs. The more units of product or service the customer produces, the more direct labor and material costs he incurs. However, not all variable costs are direct. The rental cost of additional warehouse space and the machining fluid used in the grinding operation example aren't direct costs—they are not expended for what becomes an integral part of the product or service produced. And that is the criterion for a cost to be considered direct.

Now, the reason value sellers must understand variable and fixed costs lies again in how they are perceived within the customer organization. Variable costs that are also direct costs are usually subject to tight financial controls. Direct materials, for example, are bought to cost standards, so price is an important consideration in their purchase. Their inventories and usage are planned and scheduled so that their acquisition is closely tied to their actual use or resale. The higher the dollar value of the direct materials purchased, the greater their impact is on profit and loss. Further, the higher their dollar value, the greater will be the financial and accounting influence over their source selection and the price paid for them. Generally speaking, there must be strong technical or operational considerations to justify the customer's buying high-dollar variable items on other than the lowest-price basis.

On purchases of low-dollar items whose cost is variable, the customer exercises looser controls. To begin with, if their cost is not direct, because the items purchased are not an integral part of the product or service produced, they will not be treated as inventory. That machining fluid in the grinding operation example would be an operating expense accounted for as overhead cost. Little or no effort would be made to mesh its purchase with its actual use. It would be bought in quantities convenient for purchase or storage and would be bought at convenient time intervals.

Customer controls are also loose on purchased items that are direct but, again, represent low-dollar value. For example, nuts, bolts, washers, screws, paints, and varnish may all become integral parts of a product or service, so in fact they are really direct costs. However, because they are many in number and each involves only small dollars of expenditure, they are accounted for as operating expenses and charged to overhead. The time and effort involved in capturing such costs as they are actually incurred, and charging them directly to a product, a contract, or a project, is not considered worthwhile.

Hence, on low dollar value items of variable cost, and particularly on those that are also overhead, there is low visibility. There is little application of value analysis-value engineering techniques to their specification or source of supply. There is little or no inventory planning and control of their acquisition and use. They receive only minimal negotiation and monitoring by Purchasing. And, the purchase of low-dollar items of variable cost is strongly influenced by the judgments and decisions of those who use such items in production, engineering, maintenance, and office operations.

Purchases that result in fixed costs are generally for high-dollar expenditures, such as building construction, rents, vehicle or equipment leases, insurance programs, machinery, computer and office systems, instrumentation, and laboratory and testing facilities. Such purchases have the highest visibility within the customer organization because:

- They involve large cash outlays.
- Once incurred, those outlays cannot be recovered except through depreciation allowances or the savings and increased sales those outlays produce.
- The costs of depreciation, as well as those of operating and maintaining what is bought, will be continuing costs in the future.

The process of buying fixed-cost items is typically more formalized and drawn out than that of buying production materials and services. It usually begins with an appropriation request, which is an application by some using department or activity for funds to cover the purchase of the building, machinery, or equipment it wants. The request will identify the need or objective to be satisfied, contain an estimate of the dollars to be expended, and attempt to justify the capital investment. For example:

- The request may apply simple payback analysis to show that if cost savings or increased sales recoup the capital quickly and continue beyond the payback period, the investment risk is low and the return is high.

- The request may use some more sophisticated rationale that considers not only payback analysis but also discounted cash flow. Discounted cash flow applies an interest rate to discount the cash flows resulting from the proposed investment's costs and benefits. It converts their cash values into present-time value. A high net present value is favorable for the investment; a low net present value is unfavorable.

- The request may use rate-of-return analysis, which relates the additional income or savings generated over the life of the plant or equipment to the investment outlay. It then compares the "rate of return" for the proposed investment to that rate of return used to measure total company performance. The better the investment's rate of return, the more favorable is the proposed expenditure.

Appropriation requests for capital investment generally go through several review levels before approval. The only time this review procedure may be bypassed or simplified is when the requirement is urgent. For example, critical quality problems in production may speed up the process of new equipment purchase. Increased sales, particularly large new orders, may demand immediate expansion of plant facilities. Health and safety rulings by government agencies may force immediate action to buy instrumentation and protective equipment. Under such circumstances the appropriation request may go directly to the final approval level, which in most large companies and institutions is some executive committee made up of senior operating and financial management. In smaller companies, it may be the chief executive officer and the controller or head of finance.

Salespeople selling capital equipment or services that become major elements of the customer's fixed costs must understand this review procedure and be prepared for the usually long and drawn-out time it entails. They must recognize the buying influences that get involved in the review steps. And they must also appreciate that the financial orientation of the review process can give undue importance to the price factor alone, not only because price is a major element in all evaluations of investment payback, but also because of the basic limitations of accounting systems for recognizing factors other than price in purchase decisions.

The typical accounting system doesn't make it easy for sellers to sell value. For that matter, it doesn't make it easy for customers to buy value. The accounting system, whether it be in a manufacturing, distribution, or service industry, cannot identify and capture *total costs* of a purchase as they are in fact incurred, by either item purchased or by supplier. In most cases, the accounting system captures only price and perhaps transportation and terms of payment. All other costs are hidden or disguised. They are reflected in inflated labor and processing costs, or they are aggregated into overhead accounts where their relationship to any specific item or supplier is lost completely.

Hence, to sell value, the salesperson must not only understand costs in an accounting sense but in a functional sense as well. He must have answers to questions like the following:

- What costs are a function of the customer's requirements?
- When the customer buys to satisfy those requirements, what costs are actually incurred, regardless of how they are accounted for?
- How does what we offer affect those actual costs? Does it reduce them? Does it avoid them? Does it enhance income or profit, which offsets cost?
- How does my competitor's offering affect those costs?

A Nonaccounting View of Cost

Unlike consumer buyers who may ask, "Can I afford to buy?" the industrial customer wants to know, "How much will I gain when I buy?" And the value seller helps answer that question by quantifying the cost benefits of what he sells.

To illustrate the concept of looking at costs in terms other than how they are accounted for, consider the customer's decision to buy an item of capital equipment. We saw earlier in this chapter that this decision is usually subject to a review process in which an analysis approach is used to justify the purchase. Whether the approach be discounted cash-flow analysis or rate-of-return analysis, it involves imputed costs.

Imputed costs are costs of economic rather than accounting interest and are useful to management in making decisions concerning future events. Imputed costs are (1) interest on investment and (2) opportunity costs. The first stems from the fact that when capital is spent on plant or equipment, it can't be spent, for example, on interest-bearing securities. If the interest on such securities is 10 percent and the rate of return on the equipment purchased is 20 percent, the decision to buy is a favorable one. If, on the other hand, the rate of return is only 8 percent, the difference between the 10 percent that could have been earned on securities and 8 percent must be considered a cost. It will not be accounted for as such, but it is in truth a cost.

The second type of imputed cost, opportunity cost, is involved when a customer can decide on one course of action out of a number of alternatives. For example, he can buy the new equipment or lease it; he can buy the new equipment or subcontract the operation. If the decision is to buy, then the opportunity to lease or subcontract is foregone. If either of these courses of action could have realized greater income or cost benefits than those resulting from purchase, the difference is the opportunity cost.

Obviously, salespeople selling products and services involving capital investment should thoroughly understand imputed costs because they are critical to analyzing value in the investment decision. It is entirely possible that the customer has ignored them or incorrectly allowed for them in the review process. To the extent that some omission or error undervalues the seller's offering, introducing imputed costs may be the perfect opening for value selling.

We always define value as the satisfaction of customer requirements at the lowest total cost in use. Hence, to sell value we must know what costs are a function of the customer's purchase requirements.

Costs of Satisfying Purchase Requirements

Purchase requirements are those needs that must be satisfied because the customer's products, processes, or markets demand them. Those demands can be many and varied. However, all organizations buy to satisfy two universal requirements.

The first universal requirement is for quality—design, performance, or reliability standards—which results from product, process, or market demands. Quality requirements are described by specifications, bills of material, or drawings. They are defined in terms of function or performance. Quality is achieved when what is bought meets those requirements.

The second universal purchase requirement concerns delivery and availability needs, which result from the same demands of the customer's products, processes, or markets. Delivery and availability requirements are defined by the customer in terms of delivery rates and lot sizes, completion dates, production and purchase schedules, and inventories the supplier is expected to acquire and hold. Availability is ensured by the supplier's producing in tandem with customer schedules or anticipating customer needs and producing in advance. Availability is not achieved when delivery or completion is delayed, or when quantities delivered are fewer than those ordered.

The costs of ensuring quality and delivery and availability requirements are not formally accounted for by the customer's accounting system. Yet they are real and can be recognized as such once they are identified. Although it may be difficult to quantify them for the mass of items the customer buys, they can be estimated on a discrete item-by-item basis. Probably the most important action the salesperson can take to sell value is to identify these costs to the customer, quantify them, and demonstrate their relationship to his and his competitors' offerings. Once such costs are acknowledged, the competitive criterion can no longer be price versus price alone.

Costs of Ensuring Quality

Three categories of expenditures reflect the functional relationship of cost to quality assurance. Each category includes purchase expenditures that the customer incurs to do the following:

- Prevent defects or failures before delivery or performance.
- Detect defects or failures when he physically receives what he buys.
- Correct defects or failures when what he receives does not conform to quality standards.

COSTS OF DEFECT OR FAILURE PREVENTION. Those costs incurred to avoid or reduce the incidence of failure in meeting specification requirements are, as the term implies, preventive in nature.

When the customer performs a survey of a potential supplier's physical facilities to determine his technical and production ability to supply, he incurs costs of failure prevention. Similarly, when he orders and tests samples to evaluate their suitability for his purpose, he incurs costs of failure prevention. The time and expenses of those people performing the survey or conducting the sample's evaluation may be charged against an engineering budget or accounted for in an overhead account, but the function of that time and expense is to avoid supplier failure.

Clearly, if the customer incurs expense by going through a source qualification or sample approval process to develop "competition" against an existing supplier, the price quoted by that "competition" should be factored to reflect those additional costs. If the existing supplier is already meeting specifications, the assurance of quality is achieved through his price. If the customer must perform surveys or sample approvals, the costs he incurs are real and additional to the price of the new supplier.

Another cost of prevention is the engineering time and expense involved in revising or adapting purchase specifications to compensate for shortcomings in the supplier's processes or controls. For example, growing numbers of companies are working to improve quality through statistical process controls. When they seek improvement in quality from outside suppliers, they usually must review and rewrite the specifications to which they buy. Where previously specifications covered physical properties or performance characteristics the item had to meet, they now must include detailed instructions of how the supplier must make, test, and even pack and ship the item. These measures, incurred to avoid failure, entail additional cost to the customer.

Defect or failure prevention costs are always incurred in the development of a new source. These include the time and travel expense of engineering, manufacturing, and quality control people, who must direct and monitor the new supplier's efforts in becoming an assured quality source. Failure prevention costs also include the supplier's start-up expenses for tooling or modifications in plant and equipment as well as the high scrappage and rejection rates that are typical of a start-up situation. Again, the purpose of these costs is preventive. They are incurred to avoid failure by a particular supplier in the first place.

COSTS OF DEFECT OR FAILURE DETECTION. All costs that the customer incurs to ascertain whether what he physically receives does in fact conform to what was specified, such as incoming inspection costs, are costs of failure detection. The time expended in physically weighing, measuring, and testing what a supplier delivers is a detection cost. Similarly, payments made to outside laboratories or testing agencies that certify properties or performance of what the customer has bought are costs of detection.

The fact that such costs are usually aggregated in some overhead account hides the reality that the customer incurs them unevenly with different suppliers. Even when the same items are purchased, incoming inspection costs often vary by supplier. For example, supplier A's shipments may be subjected to sample inspection using a different sample size and even a different sampling method from supplier B's. Yet the buying decision may have apportioned the business between them on the basis of price comparison alone. Further, on subsequent business, one supplier may be eliminated because his price is not "competitive." Yet, the total cost of price plus inspection in buying from him may in fact be less than that from the supplier retained.

COSTS OF DEFECT OR FAILURE CORRECTION. Costs the customer incurs because what he has physically received does not meet specifications are costs of correcting the defect or failure.

When he receives purchased goods that don't conform to specification, the customer incurs additional costs. If he needs those goods for scheduled use, he will probably inspect every unit received to separate good from bad units. If normal inspection is sampling, or merely visual, his need to perform 100 percent inspection of a more detailed nature involves additional cost.

If he rejects what he receives, he may return it to the supplier for replacement or correction. However, this generates additional cost in repacking and shipping back what he has received, re-receiving it, reinspecting it, and rehandling it. These duplications double the cost he would normally incur if what he had received initially had met required specifications. As such, they become premium—that is, extra—costs.

Both the cost of premium inspection and the cost of rejection are costs of defect or failure correction. But over and above these are the costs that become a direct consequence of the failure, as, for example:

When the customer receives defective material that must be rejected, he incurs premium costs in manufacturing. He may be forced to operate machines or production lines at less than economic levels because there is insufficient material of ensured quality to run.

When the customer starts up a vendor-designed computer system, only to find that it doesn't do what is intended, he incurs premium costs in the operational and administrative areas of his business. He may make bad or misdirected decisions because of poor information or lack of information the system generates. He may shift to manual or less efficient means of processing data because the system he bought is unreliable. He may expend all kinds of time and money to "fix" or "debug" what is faulty to begin with.

When the customer receives product from his supplier that is resold and then returned because it is defective, he incurs premium costs. At the very least, he incurs the cost of replacing what was returned. But he also could lose the sale by the order's being canceled. Conceivably, he could lose not only that one sale but future sales as well.

In all of these examples, costs are those of failure correction, and they result from the customer's not receiving what he specified and bought.

Costs of defect and failure correction are the largest costs incurred in ensuring quality. They represent on average 75 percent of total quality costs. On the other hand, less than 6 to 7 percent of all quality costs are incurred to prevent failure. This should suggest to salespeople that oftentimes the customer's view of value is shortsighted. In too many cases the customer assumes that quality is ensured from all suppliers who are "approved." Therefore, the only significant factor to consider is the competitive price alone.

The cost of ensuring quality is in theory built into the price. When the customer incurs premium costs in detecting or correcting for quality he does not get, that price does not result in value. Price is what is paid for what is specified. And clearly what the customer pays when he does not receive what he specifies is considerably more than the price itself.

Where sellers have the technical and productive capability to ensure quality more consistently and reliably than competitors, they must learn to translate such capability into terms of total cost. The old maxim that an ounce of prevention is worth a pound of cure is dramatically demonstrated when quality is considered in terms of cost.

To illustrate: It has been shown that any amount spent to prevent defects or failures at any stage of a business process will avoid tenfold costs that would be incurred otherwise.* Hence, if the customer spends an additional $100 to clarify an ambiguous purchase specification, he will save $1,000 of cost he would incur if he did not. If the customer spends $1,000 at receiving inspection to detect defective material and thereby prevent its entering his product or process, he will avoid $10,000 of cost he would incur if he did not. If the customer spends $10,000 to detect and prevent faulty products from being shipped to his customers, he will save $100,000 of cost that he would incur if he did not.

The message is clear. Quality is a customer requirement and ensuring quality entails cost. Hence, value sellers must know those costs and translate their offerings into total-quality cost terms.

COSTS OF DELIVERY AND AVAILABILITY. Costs the customer incurs to ensure that what he buys will be delivered and available in the quantities and at the time he requires them are similar to the costs he considers in making inventory planning and control decisions and reflect the functional relationship of cost to inventory control. Delivery and availability costs fall into three categories:

1. *Cost of acquisition*—the cost the customer incurs when he specifies, buys, and receives products and materials from outside suppliers
2. *Cost of possession*—the cost the customer incurs to hold, protect, and maintain what he buys up to the point of use, conversion, or sale

* This has become known as "Ison's Law of Ten." It was developed from Japanese experiences, but has been realized at companies like General Electric, Whirlpool, and others.

3. *Cost of depletion or delivery failure*—the cost of the customer's being out of stock because of delivery shortages or delays by his supplier

COSTS OF ACQUISITION. The more structured and formalized his buying process, the higher acquisition costs will be. They are typically expenditures for the following activities:

- Planning and scheduling time spent in determining purchasing quantity and delivery requirements
- Preparing and processing purchase requisitions
- Requesting and evaluating quotations from suppliers
- Placing purchase orders
- Following up and expediting orders placed
- Effecting engineering or specification changes; making amendments to the original order
- Receiving and handling what is bought
- Inspecting incoming orders; laboratory testing and certifying purchases
- Handling and moving what is received to points of use or stockrooms
- Processing invoices
- Providing clerical and data processing time and expense for all of the above activities

It is common to consider costs of acquisition as fixed, that is, not affected by the number of purchases and receivings involved. This is generally true insomuch as the customer employs the same staff and data processing facilities regardless of the number of orders placed. But this is not to say that acquisition costs are sustained uniformly, purchased item by purchased item, let alone supplier by supplier. There are purchased items that demand considerable time and expense in their purchase, follow-up, receiving, and inspecting. There are others that demand little. Similarly, there are suppliers of the same item who cause more of these acquisition costs to be incurred than do other suppliers, as, for example:

• When the customer expends twice the time with supplier A that he does with supplier B in reviewing, clarifying, and reconciling specifications and contract terms for the same item to be purchased.

• When the customer must monitor and follow up the status of open orders through frequent telephone and telefax communication, even personal visits to one supplier not required with his other suppliers.

• When the package or container size, shape, or quantity of contents from one supplier requires more time or equipment to physically handle, move, or make ready for use than that from another supplier.

Salespeople should understand how the customer incurs these acquisition costs not only on what they supply but also on what their competitors supply. Where there are significant differences in how these costs are experienced, there is an opportunity for value selling.

COSTS OF POSSESSION. These are costs that the customer incurs when inventories are created. Inventories are created when the customer acquires more than he uses or sells. They are created when he maintains reserves or protective stocks against supplier quality or delivery failures. They typically include the following:

• Rental or depreciation expense on storerooms and warehouses
• Maintenance, repair, heat, power, and light expended to operate those facilities
• Taxes on facilities and inventories
• Labor costs of handling, moving, and storing inventories
• Insurance on facilities and inventory
• Obsolescence of products, components, materials, and supplies
• Natural deterioration of products and materials with limited shelf life
• Interest paid on borrowed funds required for purchase
• Opportunity cost resulting from capital tied up in inventory rather than invested elsewhere

Although the customer makes no effort to identify or capture possession costs as they are actually incurred by purchased item or by supplier, the fact is that they are incurred differently by each criterion. Some items generate significant costs of storage and protection and are highly susceptible to early obsolescence or deterioration. Other items entail small costs and small risk. Similarly, two suppliers of the same item may easily cause the customer to incur possession costs differently and with different consequences. To illustrate:

• When a supplier prices his offerings at quantity levels over and above the customer's scheduled usage, he can cause the customer to incur additional costs. If the customer buys from that supplier, he must maintain inventories and incur the possession costs they entail. If another supplier sells in quantities that meet the scheduled demand at the same price, the customer avoids those possession costs.

• When a customer can synchronize his purchases with a supplier's scheduled production, he can avoid all costs of inventory possession. This is the meaning of "just-in-time" control that Japanese industry has employed so effectively, and which meshes the customer's requirements and the supplier's production through integrated plans and schedules. As a result, the customer's costs of possession become negligible.

• When the customer can obtain from one supplier but not another any of the following benefits, he avoids or reduces his costs of possession and incurs lower total costs in the process:

  • *Consignment*—where the supplier retains ownership of what he delivers and bills the customer only as he uses or consumes

  • *Make and hold*—where the supplier anticipates the customer's scheduled demand and produces in anticipation of it, but ships only at the customer's quantity and time instructions

  • *Systems contracting*—where the supplier takes on the responsibility of identifying the customer's inventory needs, stocking and replenishing items to satisfy those needs, and selling all that he supplies at prices reflecting total quantities rather than limited or specific items

The reality is that the customer incurs costs of possession that differ by purchased item and differ by supplier. Although the accounting system does not identify those costs and relate them accordingly, the salesperson must recognize those distinctions.

Failure to do so means the customer will compare offerings by price and price alone.

COSTS OF DEPLETION AND DELIVERY DELAYS. Customers incur some costs because a purchase is not available in the quantity required or is not delivered on time. They are the cost of being out of stock and having to compensate for that stockout or correct for the delivery failure. Costs of depletion and delay include the following:

- Expediting expense and premium transportation of delinquent deliveries
- Downtime on machines and equipment because materials are lacking
- Premium costs of manufacture or distribution because materials or product are not available to process or sell at economical quantity levels
- Man-hours wasted due to stockouts or supplier delivery delays
- Lost sales, lost goodwill, or penalties incurred because of failure to meet customer or market demands

Again, although the customer's accounting system does not acknowledge depletion and delay costs by purchased item or supplier, they are real and determinable by those criteria. To illustrate:

- Downtime on customer machines or production lines is usually accounted for in an overhead account. But the fact that it is captured and charged means that it is known or capable of being known. When downtime is the result of supplier short shipments or delivery delays, the ensuing downtime costs can be identified by item and by supplier. They are a direct consequence of a specific item's shortage and a specific supplier's failure.

- Premium costs of manufacture or distribution result when the customer is forced to produce or sell in less than economical quantities. If this occurs because the supplier has delivered less than ordered or delivered late, those premium costs are known or knowable. They are the direct result of an item's shortage and the failure of that item's supplier to supply on time.

• When the customer cannot fill an order from *his* customer because of short shipments or late delivery by his supplier, he incurs the cost of lost profit on sale. Lost profit on sale is not accounted for as a cost, but it is surely recognized by the customer as such. He knows it in dollars-and-cents terms. He knows it by item. And he knows it by the supplier who caused it.

Like the cost of ensuring quality, the cost of ensuring delivery and availability is in theory built into the price. When the customer incurs additional costs because of quantity or delivery failures by his supplier, the price is understated by those costs. It becomes, in effect, a false expression of value.

If sellers have the production, financial, and management capability to ensure delivery and availability more consistently and reliably than the competition, they should capitalize on that advantage. The key to doing so is knowing how the costs associated with availability and delivery are experienced and the premiums or savings they may involve. For example:

• The seller can reduce the customer's cost of acquisition by integrating his order-service activities with the customer's order-placement processes. This might be done by tying in his and his customer's computer and telecommunication systems. It can also be done by assigning specific personnel to speed up the customer's order placement and processing.

• The seller can reduce the customer's cost of possession by repackaging what he supplies. If he knows the specific quantities or rates that are scheduled for usage, he can ship in containers designed to hold only those specific quantities. This reduces the cost of handling and storage. It also reduces the cost of financing idle inventories.

• The seller can reduce if not eliminate the customer's cost of depletion and delay by employing the "just-in-time" controls cited earlier in this chapter. By scheduling production so that he delivers just-in-time for use, the seller ensures availability to the customer and avoids all costs of stockout and delivery failure.

Although the price quoted by the seller may be the same as a competitor's, value contributions to the customer are not the same. Value is achieved when customer requirements are satisfied at the lowest total cost. Price less savings equals lower total cost than price alone.

To assist the salesperson in selling value, there follows a glossary of accounting and nonaccounting definitions of cost. Review them and consider how your offering might avoid or reduce these costs to your customer.

Glossary of Cost-Accounting Definitions to Use in Value Selling

Costs

Costs are expenditures for material, labor and overhead (expenses) incurred in the production and sale of a product or service.

actual cost vs. standard cost Actual cost is an expenditure as it is incurred, for example, labor or material. Standard cost is a predetermined measure of cost based on time-and-motion study, past costs and production experience, expected costs, theoretical costs, or some combination thereof.

    Cost-accounting systems may employ either actual- or standard-cost data. Where the nature of the business is job-type (e.g., specialty manufacture, service, or custom trade), *actual* costs are frequently used and accounted for directly to each job or customer order. Where the nature of the business is process-type or involves the production or distribution of a broad product mix, *standard* costs are employed. These are often allocated to each process or to each unit of product.

cost accounting An orderly process of using the principles of general accounting to record the experiences of operating a business. Together with production and sales data, cost accounting enables management to ascertain production and distribution costs in a meaningful fashion.

direct costs Those costs that are incurred for, and can be identified as part of the cost of, a given product or service. Direct costs can be charged directly to a given order, job, or product. The most important direct costs are labor and materials.

direct labor The costs of all labor, performed upon the product, that changes the shape, form, or nature of the materials that enter into the product.

direct material The costs of raw materials, purchased parts, and subcontracted labor that enter into and become part of the product or service.

indirect costs   Those that do not result from the production of a specific unit of product or service and so cannot be charged directly to the product or service. They must be allocated or apportioned to it by some method of approximation.

unit costs   The cumulative costs of a unit of product incurred through the production and/or distribution cycle.

variance   Represents deviation of actual cost incurred versus standard cost. Hence, variances may be favorable (i.e., actual is less than standard) or unfavorable (the reverse).

Overhead Costs

Overhead costs are indirect costs that cannot be charged directly to a unit of product or service. They may be accounted for in one general account or may be broken down and allocated against a more directly accountable function or department. Hence, we have manufacturing, selling, administrative, and engineering overheads.

MANUFACTURING OVERHEAD

Manufacturing overhead are indirect expenses incurred in the manufacturing or conversion process. Manufacturing overhead expenses include:

Indirect labor, incurred for:
- Production departments, including foremen, group leaders, clerks, and production material handlers
- Quality control and process engineering
- Purchasing and production control, including scheduling, receiving, and stores
- Industrial engineering, supervision, cost accounting, and industrial relations

Maintenance and operating supplies and fixed or period charges (i.e., expenses not affected by quantity or volume of production)

NON-LABOR EXPENSES IN MANUFACTURING OVERHEAD

auto expenses   Cost of operating company cars and internal trucking.

depreciation and amortization   Depreciation charges for plant and equipment; amortization write-off for improvements in a leased facility.

dues, tuitions, memberships   For management and personnel.

maintenance materials   spare parts, operating and repair materials, and work performed by outside maintenance and repair contractors.

non-capital equipment and tools   Small or expendable tools (grinding wheels, files, hand tools) that are treated as expense items in a current accounting period.

obsolescence of raw material   Charges for all material scrapped, reclassified, or made obsolete.

occupancy expense   Building maintenance, depreciation, fire insurance, boiler insurance, taxes, liability insurance, and fuel and electricity.

office supplies and postage

operating supplies   Supply items generally used in the factory (gloves, cleaning rags, lubricants, coolants, etc.)

power and light   Rental charges on equipment and power bills (for ovens, motors, etc.).

telephone and telegraph

travel expense   Education expenses for seminars, plant visits, personnel moving expense, meals and lodging while on company business.

ALLOCATION OF MANUFACTURING OVERHEAD

There is no standard formula for allocating overhead, but following are common ways in which overhead may be considered.

Expense Classification	Basis of Allocation
depreciation of building	floor space occupied
depreciation of equipment	cost of machinery
fire insurance premiums	valuation of insured items
janitor services	floor or window space
supplies	estimated usage
rent of building	floor space occupied
power and light	acual material consumed
unemployment and old age and survivor's insurance	payrolls of covered employees
stockrooms	number of requisitions
payroll department	number of employees
taxes on buildings	valuation of space occupied
taxes on machinery	valuation of equipment
small tools	costs of tools used
repairs	actual cost in each department
superintendence	estimated time spent

Overhead rates may also be applied on a composited average basis (i.e., covering all indirect expenses) against a direct cost factor such as labor dollars, labor time, process time, material costs, etc.

NONMANUFACTURING OVERHEAD

Nonmanufacturing overhead includes all other indirect costs, such as selling, administrative, and engineering costs. They include research and development expenses, salesmen's salaries, commissions, travel expenses, advertising, insurance on finished goods, taxes on finished goods, officer's salaries, office personnel salaries, office stationery, legal and accounting expenses, office supplies, telephone and telegraph, losses on bad accounts and contributions.

Annual and administrative expenses are usually allocated on the basis of total cost of product (i.e., labor plus materials plus manufacturing overhead).

Other Ways of Identifying Costs for Use in Value Selling

availability costs   Costs incurred to assure availability of materials in the quantity and at the time required. Availability costs are:
- *Acquisition* Costs incurred to acquire materials, e.g., costs of purchasing and receiving
- *Possession* Costs of holding, storing, protecting materials received, e.g., costs of storage
- *Depletion* Costs of not having material as required, e.g., costs of downtime on machines because of material shortages

fixed costs   Costs not affected by production quantity or volume. They are period costs (like depreciation, rent, executive salaries) that are a function of calendar time.

imputed costs   Costs employed in making decisions concerning future events. The difference between income that can be earned on an interest-bearing security and the return on an investment in additional inventory is an imputed cost.

incremental costs   The costs of one more unit of product, labor material, etc.—the marginal cost. This is an important way to view costs, particularly in pricing out changes in work and material scope or changes in production quantity or volume. Only the incremental costs are relevant.

opportunity costs   Costs attributable to the selection of one course of action over others. The decision to buy a machine rather than lease it involves income and cost considerations. If the income benefits resulting from purchase are less favorable than those resulting from a lease, a decision to buy involves opportunity cost.

quality costs   Costs incurred to assure conformity to specifications. Costs of quality are:

- *Preventive* Costs incurred to reduce or avoid defects and failures, e.g., costs of source approval
- *Detection* Costs incurred to discover defects or failures upon receipt, e.g., costs of incoming inspection
- *Correction* Costs incurred because what has been received is defective—e.g., costs of rejection or replacement.

semi-variable   Partly variable, partly fixed, such as maintenance costs (fixed) and its overtime portion (variable).

start-up costs   A hybrid between the variable costs and fixed costs of overhead, which result from a particular project or production run. They include:

1. special engineering
   - design engineering
   - production engineering
2. special tooling—tools, dies, fixtures
3. facilities—purchase and installation of special machinery
4. rearrangement of plant
5. loss of use of facilities during setup
6. training of employees to new process or new product

Start-up costs are usually accounted for in standard overhead accounts, but can also be segregated for better control, thus avoiding their being treated as recurring rather than one-time or nonrecurring expenses.

variable costs   Those costs that vary directly with production quantity or volume—out-of-pocket costs. Other expressions of variable cost are prime cost and direct cost (direct labor and materials).

Chapter 4

IDENTIFYING AND INFLUENCING CUSTOMER REQUIREMENTS

Consumer buyers buy to satisfy needs and wants. Industrial buyers buy to satisfy requirements. Consumer needs and wants are personal. They are physical; they are psychological. They are direct expressions of each individual's concerns with survival and well-being on both the material and emotional level.

Industrial requirements are impersonal and derived. They flow from demands imposed on the company or institution by:

- The products they produce and sell and the services they perform and supply
- The processes—marketing, distribution, manufacturing, engineering, administrative—they employ to produce what they sell and supply
- The market and competitive environment in which they operate

The demands on the company require careful management of resources—manpower, time, physical facilities, materials, and capital—and technology to achieve technical, logistical, and financial performance objectives. As markets and technology change, demands change. And as demands change, customer requirements change.

Customer requirements are satisfied either internally or externally. If they are satisfied internally, the customer himself produces the product or performs the service required. If requirements are satisfied externally, the customer buys the product or service from outside suppliers and contractors. If he has the choice of satisfying requirements either internally or externally, the customer analyzes the advantages and disadvantages of each. Clearly, for our purposes we are concerned with requirements that the customer satisfies through outside purchase. Specifically, we are concerned with how those requirements are determined and how the salesperson can influence them to his advantage.

The process of determining customer purchase requirements begins with identifying and interpreting the demands from which the requirements flow.

> EXAMPLE: An assessment of the market and competitive environment shows that sales would be increased substantially if the customer added a low-priced desk copier to his existing line of office equipment.
>
> If the customer cannot build the copier himself and must buy it, a purchase "requirement" is now created. The details of that requirement are dictated by the demands of the market and competition. They will be spelled out in terms of the design and performance criteria a copier must meet; the quantities in which it can be sold; the time schedule deliveries to market must satisfy; and the price at which the copier must be sold. Since here the customer buys as a reseller, the buying influences that define the requirement are marketing and financially oriented. In terms of titles or activity, they will be marketing managers, product managers, or financial or higher management. Their specification of requirements will be in broad functional and operational terms. In all likelihood, the customer will have already identified and held discussions with a preferred supplier before the requirement is even formalized. In this scenario, the role of Purchasing would

be minimal on the matter of source selection. On repeat or follow-on purchases, however, that role could become stronger as requirements for price, delivery, or terms of payment become more important.

If the customer decides to manufacture internally, the purchase "requirement" is no longer for a desk copier but for materials, parts, and components; for manufacturing services and supplies. Requirements still flow from the demands of the market and competition, but they also flow from the demands of the product as the customer conceives and designs it. Further, because the customer is now an original equipment manufacturer (OEM), the determination of requirements becomes more drawn out and complex. More buying influences will interpret those demands, and more buying influences will reflect those interpretations in diverse judgments and decisions.

The first step in determining purchase requirements in the second scenario, where the customer decides to manufacture internally, is a product design activity that generates designs and drawings for the new copier. These will define the copier's size, configuration, power supply, circuitry, functional components, and materials, as well as give details of color, finish, and feature. In larger organizations the design activity is often performed by specialists in product engineering, components engineering, or materials engineering.

When the copier's design is completed, a bill of materials is created. This is a breakdown of the copier from its highest level of product assembly to its lowest level of raw material. The bill of materials literally defines the kinds and amounts of materials going into the copier at each level of its manufacture and assembly. Hence, the final assembly of the copier is made up of *x* quantities of subassemblies. These in turn are assembled from *y* quantities of parts and components. And these in turn are fabricated from *z* quantities of raw materials.

Concurrent with product engineering is a production or process engineering activity that defines how the copier will be produced. It defines process steps and flow, and process sequence and time. Either alone or in concert with other functions like Purchasing and Finance, Product Engineering determines what will be produced internally and what will be purchased from the outside.

Product engineering and production engineering activities are necessarily intertwined. What and how Product Engineering designs and specifies is influenced by considerations of how and where an item will be produced. Similarly, how and where it will be produced is influenced by the item's design and specifications. Items can be designed and specified either for internal manufacture or for outside purchase. For the thousands of items that cannot be produced internally, however, the question of "make or buy" never arises. They are specified initially as "buy" items to be purchased from outside suppliers.

Purchase specifications for parts and components going into the copier may be highly detailed or cursory. They may cover not only performance and materials characteristics but also process descriptions covering methods of manufacture, inspection, and quality controls. On the other hand, purchase specifications may be as brief as a designated vendor's part number. In any event, once an item is specified, it must be bought to that description. Thus, success in influencing specifications can be crucial in influencing the OEM sale.

On the basis of a sales forecast, a production control activity now develops a manufacturing plan for the copier. This plan spells out how many units must be produced at what rate and over what period of time to meet expected demand. Simultaneously, Material or Inventory Control develops a material plan, which defines how many units of purchased materials and components must be on hand to support manufacturing, the quantity and time in which they must be received, and the quantity and frequency of their reordering. This information is reflected in the form of requisitions or releases that now go to Purchasing authorizing it to buy. The package of purchase specifications and quantity and time needs constitutes the purchase requirements for the typical OEM customer.

In the case of an end-user customer, it is primarily process demands that generate purchase requirements:

- The demands of manufacturing processes create requirements for machinery, equipment, maintenance, and repair and operating supplies.

- The demands of marketing and distribution processes create requirements for advertising services, warehousing, materials handling equipment, and cars and trucks.
- The demands of engineering processes create requirements for laboratory and test equipment, technical and professional services, and engineering supplies.
- The demands of financial and administrative processes create requirements for data processing equipment, data systems and software, and insurance and specialized services.

A requirement for desk copiers typically is created by some clerical or administrative process.

End-user requirements are identified by those who manage, operate, or perform within the processes because the processes could not function unless their requirements were met. Manufacturing processes could not function if spare parts, power, and maintenance and operating supplies were not available. Distribution processes could not function if warehouse space, supplies, and fuel for cars and trucks were not available. And financial or administrative processes could not function if equipment-repair services, printing and stationery, forms, and office supplies were not available. These are the kinds of requirements that are ongoing and continuous. They involve literally thousands of individual items of purchase. In terms of total dollars of expenditure, however, they represent a small percentage of the customer's purchases.

End-user requirements are identified whenever problems within processes occur or opportunities for improvements are recognized. Common problems are

- Inability to control quality through existing machine or process controls
- Inadequate capacity to handle current or future production and sales volume
- Inefficiency or lack of cost-effectiveness of present facilities, equipment, and systems
- Inadequate control of waste or hazardous materials and environmental and safety factors

Opportunities for process improvements frequently are found in the same areas, but their identification stems from a recognition of the market and competitive advantages they offer. Opportunity-derived requirements are fewer and less frequently realized than those that are problem derived. And this fact provides a fertile field for value sellers to cultivate.

Whether end-user requirements derive from problems or opportunities, they represent relatively few individual items of purchase. In terms of dollar expenditures, however, those items represent major purchase commitments of an investment rather than expense nature. Accordingly, the procedures of authorizing and implementing their purchase differ from those for day-to-day, low-dollar items.

For day-to-day requirements, customer specifiers and users are often the same people. The purchase of these requirements is subject to loose, routine controls. Further, once the customer selects a supplier he tends to stay with that supplier until some serious and unforgiving failure occurs.

Problem- or opportunity-derived requirements are another matter. They are typically approved by an executive group or committee, and their purchase made under more formal and monitored procedures. Specifications are comprehensive and detailed, and are often developed by technical specialists other than the users. Competitive proposals are usually solicited by Purchasing and evaluated by some functional or management group. Negotiations between buyer and seller generally take place before and after bidding. They may involve questions of price, but they always involve matters of specification, performance, delivery or completion dates, and terms and conditions of purchase. The process is complex and time-consuming and poses special problems and opportunities for those who sell. Figure 4-1 lists the various purchase requirements.

Value Selling Opportunities

Now that we have reviewed how requirements are determined, where are the opportunities for you to influence that process to your advantage? And what specifically can you do to promote a sale?

Figure 4–1. Purchasing requirements by customer type.

Type of Customer	Interprets	Imposed Demands	Defines	Requirements
Reseller	→	*Market and competitive* Price, quantity/time, after sale service and support performance	→	*Commodities* Products he buys and resells
		Process Marketing and distribution, finance and administration		*Commodities* Standard equipment, operating supplies; *systems* and *services*
Original Equipment Manufacturer (OEM)	→	*Market and competitive* (Same as for reseller)	→	*Commodities* Raw materials, standard parts and components; operating, repair, maintenance, and office supplies
		Product Design, performance, reliability		*Specialty items* Parts, assemblies made to customer design
		Process Manufacturing, engineering, procurement, marketing and distribution, finance and administration		*Services* Manufacturing, engineering, financial, et al.
				Systems In all areas
End User	→	*Process* Manufacturing, engineering, distribution, finance and Administration	→	*Commodities* Maintenance, repair, operating and office supplies
				Services Specialized and professional
				Systems In all areas

It may sound like heresy, but the first thing you must do is stop focusing attention on the characteristics or details of the product or service you sell. Whenever these are mentioned or come to mind, you must immediately transpose and redefine them in terms of the customer. What are the customer's perceptions of value, and what contributions to that value can your product or service make? Specifically, you must learn to translate your offering into terms that both satisfy requirements and enable the customer to

- Reduce cost
- Avoid cost
- Offset cost through increased income or improved revenue flow

This is the real meaning of cost-effectiveness, and its pursuit is the objective of value selling. To be successful in this effort, the salesperson must be able to answer questions like the following:

Do I know and understand the demands imposed on the customer that in turn shape and define his purchase requirements? For example:

- What is the nature of his markets? Is he an OEM, a reseller, or an end user for what I sell? Who are his major competitors? Is he a cost leader and is his marketing strategy based on volume pricing or on other factors? If so, what are they?
- Are his products highly standardized commodities? Or are they engineered to meet particular customer demands? Are his products based on proprietary technology, unique design, performance, or proprietary characteristics?
- What are the processes to which my offering relates? What are the problems or constraints in those processes? Are they of a capacity, time, or efficiency nature? Does the customer acknowledge them? How about the problems he does not even recognize? What opportunities do they provide for selling value?

Do I know who the buying influences are—their names and functions, their titles, and their responsibilities and authority within the customer organization? Do I know where in the process of requirements determination and purchase they actually exercise a buying influence? Is it exercised alone or jointly with others?

Do I know how the customer uses what I sell? And how does he receive, inspect, handle, and store it? What does he expect it to do in his product, his processes, his applications? Are there other ways he can use it? Does he use it together with something else? Can they be offered together? With complementing services?

Do I know how the customer's quantity and time requirements are determined? What period of time do they cover? One month? Six months? A year? More? What are the factors he considers in planning and scheduling his requirements the way he does?

Where are the customer's costs concentrated? In what products or processes does he experience major costs? In terms of what I sell, where in those products or processes do costs cluster? At receiving inspection? In handling and storage? In actual use? How about replacement? What can be done to avoid or reduce those costs, or offset them through increased income or cash flow? Can I quantify those cost benefits either from actual cost experience or from estimates? Can I do so from the immediate customer's experience or the experience of other customers?

Let's go back to the example of the desk copier and consider what the salesperson can do to influence requirements given the scenarios we have described.

Selling to the Reseller

The purchase requirement for the resell customer is the resale product itself, a desk copier. However, before the customer can formally define that requirement in terms that allow for purchase, he must first evaluate the new-copier market and the demands he must meet to compete in it. As a reseller, the customer's evaluation will probably be done by marketing or financial management or by higher management because the questions involved are primarily of a marketing and general-business nature. They are questions about:

• Compatibility of different makes of copier with other products carried in the customer's line

- Design, performance, and feature characteristics of one make versus others
- Market or customer acceptance of each make
- Quantities available from prospective suppliers and delivery rates they can ensure
- Prices by model and quantity; prices for all models and all quantities; discounts, rebates, advertising allowances
- Terms and conditions of purchase—warranties, product service and support, terms of payment

These questions are largely ones of comparative sales potential, profit margin, cash flow, and return on investment. And they are considered in terms of specific suppliers, as well as in terms of specific copiers. Clearly, the best opportunities for selling value are at this stage of the requirements determination process, for once the customer completes this evaluation stage, he has virtually selected his source.

In selling to the reseller, the effective salesperson will make it his business to know as much as he can about the customer's markets and competition and his business plans concerning both. He will know whether those markets are industrial, commercial, institutional, or retail. He will know his customer's major customers and their buying habits: Do they buy frequently or intermittently? Do they buy for technical reasons or for price advantage alone? He will know how his own and competitive copier lines fit in with the customer's present mix and how existing markets can be expanded and new customers added. He will have estimates of incremental income the customer should enjoy at various levels of copier sales. He should have specific proposals for national or local advertising, product promotion, or direct-mail activities that the reseller can provide to increase his customer's sales.

In selling to the reseller the effective salesperson will make it his business to understand thoroughly the customer's marketing and distribution process and his financial and administrative process. He will know the customer's capacity for storing and moving existing inventories and the demands on that capacity that a new copier line will impose. He will understand the customer's procedures for sales order processing, order picking, and packing and shipping. He will learn what inventory policies and practices he employs and how frequently and in what quantities he reorders. He will make it his business to know inventory levels on existing products the customer carries and be able to recommend optimum levels for the new copier.

The salesperson should develop specific proposals on how to integrate order-placement and order-shipment procedures of reseller and customer to reduce order-processing costs. He should develop specific proposals on economical order quantities and frequencies to minimize customer carrying costs and speed up the number of inventory turns. Additionally, he should anticipate the customer's concerns about spare-parts supply and assured maintenance and service support.

The most important fact the salesperson must understand is that the resell customer provides basically a logistical and financial function in the markets he serves. He carries the range and mix of inventories that his customers are not willing or able to carry. He fills customer demands in quantities and frequencies uneconomical for them to consider. He bridges a gap in their cash flow, by supplying materials and products at favorable terms of payment. And he must do all this at competitive resale prices. His perceptions of value, therefore, must necessarily be in cost and financial terms. And because price is a major factor in his income and profit-loss considerations, he will understandably be acutely conscious of the price he pays for what he buys. It should be no surprise that resale markets are highly price sensitive.

But price is only one element of the reseller's cost. As a provider of mostly logistical and financial services, he incurs significant costs. In Chapter 3 we refer to such costs as the costs of availability and delivery. They are the costs the customer incurs in acquiring and holding inventories, the costs he incurs when he lacks inventory to satisfy his customer demands. They are the high costs of money tied up in the inventory investment and in interest payments he makes to keep that inventory current and active.

The effective salesperson will know his customer's business well enough to understand and discuss availability and delivery costs in detail. He will know his own products and services intimately enough to relate them to the customer in terms of those costs. He will not ignore price, but will place it in the correct perspective of its being one cost among others. He will sell value by addressing both the customer's requirements and the total costs involved in satisfying them. In specific terms he will show how his offering succeeds in:

- Reducing costs
- Avoiding cost
- Offsetting cost through increased income or improved cash flow

Selling to the OEM

When the customer is an OEM who produces the desk copier himself, his requirements are for the materials and components that go into that copier. They are for plastic and aluminum parts, power supply units, switches, relays, wire and cable, and hundreds of other items, which will all be specified in technical terms at some design engineering stage. The precise definition of those technical requirements will reflect the demands of the product itself as it is conceived at the product design level. Thus, the design, performance, and other characteristics of the copier dictate the specifications of its major components. And these in turn dictate the specification of the parts and materials that go into these components.

Although market and competitive considerations strongly influence the design of the copier itself, they become less significant factors in the requirements-determining process thereafter. Whereas marketing and technical managers spelled out the requirements the copier must meet to sell competitively, engineers and technicians spell out the requirements of its materials and components. They do so from a purely technical orientation rather than a marketing or competitive one. They design and specify from what has been tried and proved. In some instances their design or specification choices are discretionary. In most cases, however, they are constrained by considerations of:

- Company, industry, or professional standards for materials, dimensions, tolerances, and other features that must be met in design and specification decisions

- Lack of information concerning design or specification options that are applicable and available
- Lack of sources who are qualified to meet requirements
- Lack of funding or time to qualify new sources
- Professional conservatism toward experimenting at the design stage
- Personal reluctance to take the risks of deviating from the tried and proved

To influence specifications favorably, the salesperson selling to the OEM must know and understand where and how what he sells is or could be used in the customer's product and how critical the function it performs is to the customer's application. Clearly, the more critical the function to the customer's product performance, market acceptance, or competitive uniqueness, the more its specifications will reflect those considerations. Thus, if the uniqueness of the copier is the customer's exclusive incorporating of the toner, the drum, and the developer into one replaceable cartridge, that cartridge is critical to the copier's sales. And if the cartridge is a purchased component of the copier, its design and specification requirements must be considered in the initial product design stage.

At the design stage the buying influences are marketing, as well as technically, oriented. They are managers of marketing and design engineering, product planners, and project managers. And their perceptions of value are in marketing and technical terms. This is the level that the salesperson must reach, and it is in terms of those value perceptions he must present his offering.

Conversely, the function of the fasteners, resistors, dials, and switches are not critical to the copier's performance, market acceptance, or competitive uniqueness. Hence, their design and specification will not reflect such considerations. Rather, they will reflect the opinions and judgments of engineers and technical specialists who are at lower levels in the requirements-determining process. They also will reflect personal and impersonal considerations, such as the ones cited above—habit, indifference, lack of knowledge of alternatives, lack of time to consider alternatives, lack of approved or qualified sources, constraints of standards, and unwillingness to experiment with what is not tried and proved. It may come as a distinct shock to those who sell in OEM markets to learn that considerations such as these play such an important role in determining design and specification requirements. But the fact is they do.

Influencing the OEM's Definition of Requirements

Favorably influencing the definition of requirements of the OEM customer involves a three-step exercise in which each step is taken in sequence. First, the salesperson must know where in the requirements-determining process the decision will be made as to how those requirements are defined. Who specifically, by function or title, are the buying influences? Who will do the actual design or specification writing for what you sell? As a general rule, the more critical the function the item performs in the customer's product, the more the decision about who will design or write the specifications will be a carefully analyzed and evaluated one. It will reflect not only technical considerations but considerations of cost, availability, and market and competitive ramifications. The less critical the function, the more likely the decision will be made solely by the specification engineer and for reasons that range from the purely technical to the personal, such as specifying from habit or specifying to "play it safe."

Salespeople should learn to apply a simple value analysis technique to determine the criticalness or importance of what they supply to the customer's product. They should think function. They should ask themselves:

- What function does my product or service perform that in turn enables the customer's product to function as it is intended?
- If the customer's total functional value is 100 percent, what percentage of that total does my offering contribute?

In the example of the replaceable cartridge combining toner, drum, and developer, it would not seem unreasonable to ascribe a value contribution of 10–12 percent for that cartridge toward the functional value of the copier as a whole.

The second step in influencing the definition of requirements of the OEM customer is to address the specific considerations that are apt to be reflected by those who decide design and specification requirements. To illustrate:

- If the item to be purchased is critical to the customer's product performance, request a meeting with his key technical people for the distinct purpose of performing an analysis of your offering as it relates to his product application. By identifying the functional demands of his product, demonstrate how your product features, properties, and performance characteristics best satisfy those functional demands. If the demand is for simplicity of operation, demonstrate what in your product's design best satisfies that objective. If the demand is for ease of maintenance, why is it achieved best through your offering.¹

- If the specifier is reluctant to consider your product or offering because he is unfamiliar with it, present case histories that show successful experience in similar applications. Quote facts and figures that bear out your claim. Cite testimonials and documentation from other satisfied customers, from professional and independent third-party sources.

- If requirements are defined in narrow or limited terms and this is to your disadvantage, point out to the specifier the benefits of a broader definition. For example, metal parts may be currently machined by one supplier, heat treated by another, plated by another, and assembled by still another. Each purchase demands separate drawings and specifications that entail not only additional engineering expense but also an increased risk of quality failure. When you, the seller, have the resources and capability, show the customer benefits in "scaling up." Instead of specifying parts, specify assemblies. Instead of specifying by materials or design description, specify in terms of function. Instead of specifying products, specify systems. In brief, demonstrate the benefits of added value contribution to the customer by specifying around your strengths and your expertise.

The third and final step needed to influence the OEM's definition of requirements is to quantify in cost terms the benefits to the customer by defining design and specification requirements as you propose they be defined. Again, the cost benefits include the cost avoidance that results from ensured quality; the cost savings and cost avoidance that result from lower inventories and ensured supply, as needed; and the cost offsets that result from improved cash flow and return on inventory investment because of faster inventory turns and fewer inventory stockouts.

Your task as a value seller is to relate your offerings to the customer's requirements in cost-effective terms. To do this, you must make it your business to know shop superintendents, production foremen, inspection and quality control people, and production control supervisors and learn firsthand from them what their experience has been with your and your competitors' products. Where that experience is reflected in costs as accounted for, you should find out what they are. Where no accounting data are available, you should estimate costs. For example, if the customer's production experience shows that your rate of quality failure is half that of your competitor, what does this mean in cost terms? What is the difference in time spent in incoming inspection or in actual production to detect defective units and to correct for their occurrence? At some reasonable estimate of dollars for time spent, what is the comparative cost of quality failure between your competitor and you?

Again, if your on-time delivery performance is 95 percent and your competitor's is only 75 percent, what are the cost consequences to the customer of that 20 percent difference? How is it manifested to him in terms of expediting costs, lost production time, premium cost of manufacture? How is it manifested in terms of lost orders or lost profit on sales? Value to the customer is total cost in use, and when you are selling to the OEM customer, it is critical for both you and him to acknowledge costs in use.

Selling to the End User

Favorably influencing the definition of requirements of the end-user customer depends in large measure on the size and significance of the transaction. For example, if the purchase of a desk copier is a single-unit, one-time purchase, the buying influences and their perceptions of value are one situation. If the purchase is for the customer's total companywide requirements, or for a continuing and recurring demand, the situation is something else.

In the case of the one-time purchase, the office manager or manager of the department in which the copier is used is probably its specifier. His perceptions of value are derived from the problems or opportunities he recognizes in his clerical and administrative processes. Is he currently having trouble generating copies fast enough to keep up with the demands of Accounts Receivable, Order Entry, and Customer Service? Is he limited in the sales promotion or advertising he can do because of the number, size, and varieties of copies he can make? Are there opportunities for expanding business or marketing activities with a speedier, more efficient, more versatile copier?

If the copier is a single-unit, one-time sale, influencing the definition of its requirement and specifications and determining the seller who will supply it are often one and the same exercise. This is because the demands of the customer's clerical processes dictate his requirements in the copier. And the requirements of the copier are essentially requirements of function. These in turn are satisfied or not satisfied by design and performance features in each copier under consideration. It is the task of the salesperson to show how the copier he sells best meets those functions and performance requirements. Perhaps material and design features of his copier enable the user to produce so many copies per minute at so many cents per copy. They allow the user to load a fresh supply of paper in a minimum amount of time. They allow him to feed paper automatically and switch from one copy size to another semiautomatically. These performance results generate cost savings or cost avoidances that are real and quantifiable. They may be significant enough to justify a premium cost in the price of the copier itself.

If the purchase of copiers is a large one, involving the customer's total company needs, the requirements-specifying process will be more time-consuming and complex. It will involve a coordinating effort among customer-using activities to specify and define copier specifications uniformly for all using locations. It will involve a budgetary planning and control exercise that sets targets or ceilings on what can be expended by each location where copiers are used. It will involve a formal process of bid solicitation, evaluation, and negotiation in which personnel in Purchasing and Finance will play an active role together with those from the using and specifying activities.

The specifying of the copier will be a largely technical process, as will the determination of which suppliers are best qualified to supply it. Once quotations are solicited and received, however, the evaluation of responses becomes more than a mere technical exercise. If it is a two-step evaluation process, suppliers will be rated first on technical considerations by specifying or using personnel. They will be rated on factors such as understanding of the specifications, copier design and performance characteristics, after-sale services, and support available. Step two of the evaluation process will be an assessment by Purchasing and Finance of comparative prices, transportation charges, terms of payment, discounts, and terms and conditions of sale, including acceptance, warranties, and remedies for nonperformance.

If evaluation is a one-step process, both technical and business considerations will be evaluated at the same time.

Clearly, if the salesperson seeks to influence specification requirements to his advantage, he must do so early in the requirements-determining process. He must convince both specifier and user that their requirements are best met by specifying around his unique design and performance characteristics. He must show how those characteristics satisfy the customer's clerical and administrative needs. And he must demonstrate that they not only satisfy those needs but also generate cost savings, cost avoidances, or cost offsets that justify a higher technical evaluation than that afforded by competitive copiers.

If the salesperson cannot relate his product and service features to the customer's process requirements in terms of cost-effectiveness, it will be difficult for the end user to justify the purchase on a basis other than the competitive price.

Chapter 5

THE VALUE SELLING STRATEGY CHECKLIST

Value is the satisfaction of customer requirements at the lowest total cost in use. Value contribution is a product or service feature or benefit that:

- Satisfies a customer requirement
- Reduces customer cost, avoids it, or offsets it through improved income or revenue flow

Value contributions are acknowledged or perceived by the customer. If they are acknowledged, the customer directly relates them to the satisfaction of his requirements. He also evaluates them in terms of the experienced or expected cost benefits that flow from those features or benefits. More favorable terms of payment, for example, are an acknowledged value contribution.

Value contributions are also perceived. If they are perceived, the customer might make the same buying decision he would if he acknowledged them. However, value contributions that are only perceived are rarely related to requirements satisfaction in cost-benefit terms. More attractive packaging is an example of a perceived value contribution. When value contributions are only perceived, the requirements-cost relationship is either assumed or ignored. This entails the risk that the customer might place less importance or even ignore perceived value contribution because of the acknowledged advantage of a lower competitive price. Thus, value contributions that are acknowledged weigh more heavily towards a favorable buying decision than those that are only perceived.

Not all product and service features and benefits contribute value as we have defined that term. The bright, glossy finish on the fractional horsepower motor you sell may add to its appearance and make it a benefit the customer might like to have, but if the motor is encapsulated within your customer's product frame or chassis assembly and is never seen by his customer, the aesthetics of a bright, glossy finish contribute no value as we understand that concept. Certainly a finish that prevents corrosion and adds to the motor's service life contributes value, but the aesthetics of that finish do not unless the customer's market demands it.

Nevertheless, because buying influences are at times impressed with features and benefits that are not direct value contributions, you should recognize them for what they are and factor them into your selling strategy.

In the order of their importance to a favorable buying decision, we have the following customer views of value contribution.

1. *Value contribution that is acknowledged.* The customer recognizes its validity; agrees it satisfies requirements directly; and relates it to experienced or expected cost benefits.
2. *Value contribution that is perceived.* Here the customer is aware of the relationship between the feature or benefit and the satisfaction of his requirements. However, he does not or cannot quantify that relationship in cost-benefit terms.
3. *Features or benefits that the customer might like to have for prestige or aesthetic reasons.* In terms of satisfying the cus-

tomer's requirements, they provide no direct value contribution.

4. *A product or service feature that contributes no value and provides no benefit the customer acknowledges.* This is therefore an unfavorable factor in the buying decision.

In developing a value selling strategy, you must assess your product features and service capabilities as the customer acknowledges or perceives them. This is the real meaning of being customer-oriented, and value selling is always a customer-directed process.

But value is a relative concept. The customer's acknowledgment or perceptions of value are developed by comparison. They are influenced by competition. What the customer recognizes as a value contribution is only meaningful if the offerings of one supplier can be compared with those of another. Hence, value selling must be not only customer-oriented but competition-oriented as well.

In developing a value selling strategy you must make as objective an assessment as possible of how you measured up competitively. How do your product or service features or benefits satisfy customer requirements compared with competition's? How do they provide cost benefits to the customer compared with competition's? On any value contributing feature or benefit, is your offering clearly superior to that of competition's? Is it better or more advantageous than most? Is it only on a par with competition's? Is it inferior or less advantageous than competition's? Obviously, the more favorable our competitive standing in contributing value as seen by the customer, the greater is the likelihood of your sales success.

At the conclusion of this chapter is a Value Selling Checklist (shown in Table 5-1) that you can use to develop a value selling strategy. It should be considered at every step in the requirements-determining process because what may be ignored or acknowledged as a value contribution at one step in that process may be recognized and acknowledged at another. Similarly, the checklist should be used in formulating the selling approach to any and all buying influences. What may not be seen or understood as a value-cost relationship by one influence may be easily identified and quantified by another. Thus, the checklist can become an important tool for developing an effective value selling plan and presentation.

The Value Selling Checklist relates specific product and service features or benefits to customer value contributions as follows:

- As the customer acknowledges or perceives that relationship
- As our offering compares competitively to other seller offerings

In their order of favorable impact on the sale, the checklist ranks value contributions as seen by the customer as follows:

1. The customer acknowledges product or service value contribution and understands its relationship to cost savings, cost avoidance, and cost offsets.
2. The customer perceives a value contribution but does not or cannot see its relationship to experienced or potential cost improvement.
3. The customer recognizes a benefit, but not one directly related to product, process, or market—or competition-imposed requirements.
4. The customer sees no benefit and no value contribution, direct or indirect, to the satisfaction of his requirements.

The Value Selling Checklist also assesses value contributions as they are available in competitive offerings. In supplying them, how do you compare with competition? In terms of value contribution, how do your product and service features or benefits rate? In their order of advantage to the value seller, the checklist rates these as follows:

1. Value contributions in our product and service offerings are clearly superior to those that the customer can acquire from competitive offerings.
2. They are better than those available from most competitors, but not clearly superior to any.
3. They are only average—no better but no worse than competition.
4. They are inferior, not on a par with those offered by competition.

The Value Selling Checklist identifies value contributing product and service features that satisfy customer requirements with cost benefits. Low price is indeed an important cost benefit to the customer, and the value seller cannot ignore it. But the customer's bottom-line consideration should be total cost in use. It is the task of value selling to relate product and service features to customer requirements with cost-effectiveness.

In using the Value Selling Checklist, you should first list those product or service features in your offering that relate directly to the customer's specified requirements. For example:

• The customer specifies that the outdoor lighting fixtures he wants to install must be cost-effective to operate and maintain. A feature of your fixtures is that they are of the disconnecting, lowering type, which means they are controlled independently from ground level and can be lowered and raised for servicing. This simplifies maintenance. An additional feature is that your fixtures have deep canopies into which the lamps are recessed, and this provides protection to both fixture and connections from the danger and damage of inclement weather.

• The customer specifies that the seller shall maintain sufficient inventories to satisfy quantity and delivery requirements as customer forecasts and schedules dictate. Seller shall ship only on authorized order release. An important feature of your distribution operation is that you have computerized all planning, scheduling, and inventory control. You place computer terminals in customer facilities, allowing requisitioners not only to order directly but also to know real-time status of quantities shipped, on hand, and on order. Because of your size and financial resources, you carry 50,000 line items in sufficient quantity to satisfy all foreseeable demand. Additionally, you have the capability to pick and pack discrete items into ready-to-assemble kits.

• The customer specifies that the computer diskette he buys must meet a zero defect requirement. A feature of your diskette manufacturing process is that you inspect production units more than 100 times as they move down the production line. You test them to performance levels that are higher than industry standards. You also certify that each unit the customer receives is 100 percent error-free.

After listing your product or service features that relate directly to the customer's requirements, rate those features first in terms of how the customer acknowledges or perceives their value contribution, and second, in terms of how they measure up against competitive offerings. Where your product or service offering contains no feature that directly relates to a specified requirement, the checklist notes that fact accordingly. Obviously, on that requirement factor your rating is an unfavorable one.

Not all customer requirements, however, are expressly specified. In more cases than not they are implied in the specifications themselves. For example, when the customer specifies a design or performance objective, it is an implied requirement that the selected supplier have a technical and physical staff capable of meeting that objective. When the customer specifies a configuration or tolerance, it is an implied requirement that the supplier have the machines and tools capable of meeting that specification. Implied requirements are typically satisfied by supplier capabilities.

Again, requirements are not expressly specified when the customer assumes that the capabilities needed to satisfy implied requirements already exist. This occurs when the customer approves or qualifies sources as a condition for bidding. He now assumes that his requirements can be satisfied by the sources approved. Although his requirements may in fact be unique and so demand unique capabilities to satisfy, his specifications as written actually ignore that fact. To illustrate:

• Two suppliers with the same equipment may be similarly approved to produce parts that meet customer-specified shapes or dimensions. However, one supplier uses manufacturing and quality controls that satisfy that requirement with greater reliability than the other. The first supplier's process achieves one defect in one hundred; the second achieves one defect in thirty.

• Again, two suppliers may have the same number of offices and comparable professional staffs to provide financial and banking services. However, one has data processing and telecommunication facilities that can handle customer instructions more quickly and in greater detail. The same one also has information and control systems that provide the customer with greater flexibility in maintaining, investing, and transferring funds.

These differences in capability, however, may in fact be ignored by the way specifications are expressly defined.

When the customer ignores or cannot see supplier capability differences, he tends to buy on the basis of competitive price alone. Accordingly, it is precisely those capability differences that the value seller must identify and relate to customer value contribution. The Value Selling Checklist does this by addressing not only features and benefits but also capabilities that truly satisfy customer requirements.

Quality and availability requirements are expressly defined in terms of specifications, delivery quantities, and delivery rates. However, implied in those expressly stated requirements are other requirements for supplier capabilities. Such capabilities are technical, professional, managerial, and financial. They contribute value in the form of activities, practices, controls, systems, and information that relate directly to the customer's specified needs. They contribute value because they reduce cost, avoid cost, or offset cost. Following in more detail is a representative list of quality and availability capabilities that the Value Selling Checklist addresses.

Quality-Assurance Related Capabilities

Engineering services and resources—Includes the professional experience and educational level of your people in design engineering, manufacturing engineering, and field service engineering. It considers the specialization and flexibility in engineering disciplines that you can supply to design, specify, produce, and support what the customer requires. It may also include facilities where these are relevant.

Engineering controls—Considers the systems you have in place to control engineering changes, drawings, material substitutions, and engineering schedules. It may include value engineering capabilities to meet customer design objectives at lower cost.

Tooling control—Considers the tool control system and methods of maintaining accountability for customer tools and those held by vendors and subcontractors. It considers your ability to alter or modify tooling effectively when the customer requires specification or process changes.

Manufacturing (or other operational) processes—Refers to those elements of machine and manpower production that most directly relate to the customer's quality requirements. They include:

- The use of statistical process controls at critical points in the production process
- Standards and control of standards over productivity, workmanship, machine operation, and maintenance
- The use of computer-assisted machines and tooling to achieve quality objectives

Procurement controls—Refers to procurement policies, practices, and procedures used to control vendor and subcontractor quality performance. The elements considered are the same as those addressed in number 4, except that they relate to control over outside sources.

Quality controls—Considers the following:

- Organization of quality control and quality assurance activities
- The nature and type of inspection and test procedures
- Sampling plans and methods of establishing and meeting acceptable quality levels
- Receiving inspection controls
- Raw material and stock control—rotation of stock identification and disposition of obsolete materials, control of materials with short shelf life or susceptibility to deterioration
- Assembly and fabrication controls—practices and procedures for maintaining good workmanship, good housekeeping, and effective maintenance and calibration of tools, dies, and fixtures
- Information systems and data capturing procedures for:
   —Identifying defective products and materials
   —Analyzing the nature and causes of failure
   —Taking corrective action to prevent failure the next time
- Final test and acceptance procedures

Packaging, packing, and shipping controls—Deals with the standards and practices used to protect the product quality in packing and shipping; to ensure accuracy of markings on interior and exterior packages and containers; and to ensure accuracy of shipping documents.

Reliability engineering—Considers those activities and practices aimed at improving product quality by analyzing test and failure data and recommending corrective action.

After-sale service and support—Considers the following:

- Ability to supply parts and services as the customer requires them

- Availability of parts and service centers at locations convenient to the customer
- Ability to provide preventive maintenance on a continuing basis
- Availability of literature, seminars, and training and refresher programs to instruct customer personnel in operation and maintenance procedures
- Product warranties, service guarantees

Product improvement—Refers to those research and development projects, programs, or activities that are specifically designed to improve product quality, reliability, or performance levels. To be a meaningful factor of value contribution, only those product improvement efforts that relate to the customer's requirements should be considered.

Availability Capabilities

Physical facilities and capacity (production, distribution, and other)—Refers to manpower—production or professional—machinery, equipment, and other physical facilities to produce what the customer specifies. It refers to their quantity and mix, capacity, productivity, and ability to expand as requirements dictate.

Outside sources to complement or expand capabilities and capacities—Refers to your ability to increase production or supply through purchase or subcontract agreement or through licensing and cross-licensing, franchise, agency, or other arrangements.

Physical location of facilities—Considers where plants, offices, warehouses, distribution points, and sales and service centers are located to ensure on-time delivery or on-schedule completion of customer requirements.

Production planning, scheduling, and control capabilities—Refers to the planning, scheduling, and control system used to meet customer quantity and time demands. If it is computerized, it provides advantages in:

- Forecasting customer requirements and planning production to satisfy them
- Scheduling and loading machines and manpower to accommodate customer demands for product variations in performance, size, color, and mix
- Monitoring production to provide real-time status of orders received and in process and orders completed or in transit to the customer

- Handling changes flexibly in quantities or delivery and satisfying short-notice demands
- Following up and expediting where necessary

Inventory controls—Refers to the policies and practices, systems and procedures that determine how much inventory will be carried; in what quantities it will be replenished; and the frequency with which it will be replenished. It addresses both our capability and willingness to:

- Anticipate customer requirements and produce orders in advance
- Hold inventories in anticipation of customer orders
- Hold inventories on all products by all product variations
- Consign inventories
- Rotate inventories by replacing older stock items with newer or more updated ones; eliminate obsolete items

Customer order processing and administration—Refers to systems and procedures for receiving, processing, and scheduling customer orders. It refers to those features that ensure speed of processing, accuracy in their implementation, and a quick and easy means of follow-up. It refers to those capabilities we have in contract, project, or program management and administration that help ensure promised delivery or completion date.

Traffic and transportation capabilities—Considers the physical means of transportation we own or lease to deliver materials and products to customers. It includes the scheduling, routing, and monitoring systems to use those means effectively. It also includes the information and reports we generate to inform customers of their shipment status.

Features, benefits, and capabilities are direct value contributions because they satisfy customer requirements, both specified and implied, and do so with cost-effectiveness. There are other factors, however, that can influence the buying decision, and in the Value Selling Checklist we call these "other value considerations." The checklist identifies those that are relevant to the sale and rates them by the same criteria as it rates the other factors.

Other Value Considerations

Reputation—general and specific—Includes considerations such as the general estimation in which we are held by the marketplace as a whole and the specific reputation we have among buying influences for product quality, product delivery, quality of management, cooperativeness, fairness, loyalty, ethical conduct.

Customer constraints—Refers to factors that limit or qualify, favor or prejudice the customer's choice of source or supplier. It refers to situations where the customer's customer specifies the source or expresses clear preference for one over others. It refers to situations where government regulations, health and safety standards, and environmental or other circumstances influence the customer's selection or evaluation of source.

Legal considerations—Pertains to matters of contract and contract law—our terms and conditions of sale, their terms and conditions of purchase. Are they compatible or acceptable to buyer and seller? It also pertains to methods and forms of contracting and pricing formulations; again, their compatibility and acceptability to buyer or seller.

Miscellaneous—Any other factor the salesperson can identify and recognize as a value consideration to the customer.

Value Selling Checklist

Let us now review the Value Selling Checklist shown in Table 5-1. In the first column we list customer requirements as they are expressly defined or specified. To enhance their meaning, the salesperson might weigh the importance of each requirement as he thinks the customer evaluates it. When requirements that are expressly specified have been considered, the salesperson should then consider those requirements that are implied. They are for quality and availability assurance. Again, depending on the weight he attributes to specified requirements, he then assigns proportionate weights to the implied ones.

In the second column the salesperson matches value contributing product and service features to customer-specified requirements. He should attempt to relate feature to requirement on as direct a basis as he can. Following this, he matches those quality and availability capabilities that he believes contribute value toward satisfying the customer's implied requirements. Again, he should

(text continues on page 86)

Table 5-1. Value Selling Checklist.

Customer Requirements	Value Contributions	Customer Assessment of Value	How Do We Measure Up?
[Specified and implied] *[Weighted as to importance to the customer]*	• Product and service features • Benefits and capabilities that satisfy requirements with cost-effectiveness	• Acknowledges • Perceives • Sees benefit • Sees no value	• Clearly superior • Better than most • On a par • Inferior
Example 1 Outdoor lighting fixtures must be cost-effective.	• Fixtures are disconnecting and lowering in design. • Deep canopies for protection of fixtures and connections.	Acknowledges Acknowledges	Clearly superior Better than most
Example 2 Power supply package must withstand crash impact of *x* pounds and still function.	• Working components are shielded by protective materials.	Perceives	Clearly Superior
Example 3 Seller must maintain sufficient inventory to meet forecast and schedules.	• We have computerized controls. • We carry large inventories. • We have a parts kitting capability.	Assign rating	Assign rating

Customer Requirements	Value Contributions	Customer Assessment of Value	How Do We Measure Up?
List other customer-specified requirements.	• Identify product and service features.	Assign rating	Assign rating
	• Benefits and capabilities that directly relate to requirements and reduce costs, avoid costs, and offset costs.	Assign rating	Assign rating
	Identify where no product or service feature satisfies a customer requirement.	Unfavorable rating	Unfavorable rating
Customer requirements not specified expressly			
Quality Assurance Requirements:	• Engineering services capabilities	Assign rating	Assign rating
	• Engineering controls	Assign rating	Assign rating
	• Equipment and tooling controls	Assign rating	Assign rating
	• Manufacturing and operating controls	Assign rating	Assign rating
	• Procurement controls	Assign rating	Assign rating
	• Quality controls		
	(a) Organization	Assign rating	Assign rating
	(b) Inspection/ test	Assign rating	Assign rating

(continued)

Table 5–1.   (Continued)

Customer Requirements	Value Contributions	Customer Assessment of Value	How Do We Measure Up?
Quality Assurance Requirements:	(c) Sampling and AQL	Assign rating	Assign rating
	(d) Receiving inspection	Assign rating	Assign rating
	(e) Material and stock control	Assign rating	Assign rating
	(f) Assembly and fabrication control	Assign rating	Assign rating
	(g) Information systems and procedures	Assign rating	Assign rating
	(h) Final test and acceptance	Assign rating	Assign rating
	• Packaging, package and shipping controls	Assign rating	Assign rating
	• Reliability engineering	Assign rating	Assign rating
	• After-sale service and support		
	(a) Parts and service as needed	Assign rating	Assign rating
	(b) Location of parts and service centers	Assign rating	Assign rating
	(c) Preventive maintenance on continuing basis	Assign rating	Assign rating
	(d) Customer training in operation and maintenance	Assign rating	Assign rating

Customer Requirements	Value Contributions	Customer Assessment of Value	How Do We Measure Up?
	(e) Product warranties, service guarantees	Assign rating	Assign rating
Quantity/Time Assurance (Availability Capability)	• Physical facilities and capacity	Assign rating	Assign rating
	• Outside sources to complement capability and capacity	Assign rating	Assign rating
	• Physical location of facilities	Assign rating	Assign rating
	• Production controls		
	(a) Forecasting and planning capability	Assign rating	Assign rating
	(b) Scheduling and loading for product variations and mix	Assign rating	Assign rating
	(c) Ability to monitor customer orders for real-time status	Assign rating	Assign rating
	(d) Flexibility in handling changes and short notice demands	Assign rating	Assign rating
	(e) Follow-up and expediting	Assign rating	Assign rating

(continued)

Table 5–1. *(Continued)*

Customer Requirements	Value Contributions	Customer Assessment of Value	How Do We Measure Up?
Quantity/Time Assurance (Availability Capability)	• Inventory		
	(a) Able to anticipate customer demand	Assign rating	Assign rating
	(b) Able and willing to hold customer inventories	Assign rating	Assign rating
	(c) Full product line	Assign rating	Assign rating
	(d) Will consign	Assign rating	Assign rating
	(e) Rotation of inventory	Assign rating	Assign rating
	• Customer order processing and administration	Assign rating	Assign rating
	• Traffic and transportation capabilities	Assign rating	Assign rating
Other Value Considerations	• Reputation— general and specific	Assign rating	Assign rating
	• Customer constraints	Assign rating	Assign rating
	• Legal considerations	Assign rating	Assign rating
	• Other considerations—identify	Assign rating	Assign rating

attempt to relate these capabilities directly to satisfying those requirements.

In the third column the salesperson evaluates the customer assessment of value contribution in those product and service features and those supplier capabilities he has identified.

In the fourth column, the salesperson evaluates how he compares with competitors in providing value contribution as the customer assesses it. He makes that comparison product feature by product feature, capability by capability.

How to Use the Value Selling Checklist

The Value Selling Checklist identifies how product features and service capabilities satisfy customer requirements, competitively. To complete the value selling exercise, however, you must demonstrate that relationship in cost terms. To the best of your ability, you must show the cost-effectiveness of your offering. How do product and service features and benefits reduce cost, avoid cost, and offset cost to the customer?

Again, the Value Selling Checklist provides the basis for showing that relationship. To illustrate this step, let's go back to the three examples that introduce the checklist shown in Table 5-1.

For each factor of customer requirement and value contribution (columns 1 and 2), you will enter cost as you know it or can estimate it:

- As it is experienced or likely to be experienced by the customer
- As it will be reduced, avoided, or offset by our offering

Then you will pencil in these numbers under the ratings assigned in columns 3 and 4. Thus, to cost-justify the examples, proceed as follows:

- Example 1 states that a specified requirement for outdoor lighting fixtures is that they must be "cost-effective." A feature of our product is that the fixture can be lowered and raised from the ground for easy servicing. From the customer's own experience, the labor time to service his existing fixtures is 20 man-hours/unit/yr. The lowering and raising feature of our fixtures reduces that time by 6 man-hours/unit/yr. At a labor cost of $25/hr., this feature reduces the annual cost of maintenance from $500 to $350. This is an annual reduction of $150/unit. On the checklist, next to "fixtures are disconnecting . . .," pencil in $ under "acknowledges" (column 3) and $ under "clearly superior" (column 4).

• But our fixture has another feature. Its deep canopies provide constant protection from damage caused by inclement weather, which has caused outages at least once on 7 percent of the fixtures installed during the past year. We estimate the costs of replacement and repair, plus the cost of additional lamp and connector inventories, we estimate an additional cost to the customer of $98/unit/yr. Next to "deep canopies," in column 3, insert this number. In column 4, insert "better than most." Thus, we note that our fixtures can reduce customer cost by $150 and $78, or $228/unit/yr. on these two features alone.

• We know from Example 2 that the customer requirements call for a power supply package able to withstand a specified crash-impact load. A feature of our product is its shock-resisting shield that provides even greater protection than the customer specifies. Assuming that the customer only perceives this feature as a real value contribution, let's translate what we know into cost terms.

• Past failure rates of the power supply package from impact damage were 5 percent of lot quantities reeived. The annualized costs of these failures we estimate as follows:

• Premium inspection and rejection—350 man-hours at $10/hr. or $3,500
• Re-receiving, rehandling, reinspecting—200 man-hours at $10/hr. or $2,000
• Manufacturing losses due to defective units (schedule delays, less than economical runs, lost assembly time)—400 man-hours at $12/hr. or $4,800
• Spoilage and waste (scrapped material)—$1,200
• Cost of additional inventory to cover losses—$3,600

Insert these numbers under the customer's perceived assessment of value (column 3). They total $15,100.

The protective shielding in our unit eliminates impact damage completely. Thus, its cost-effectiveness is a reduction to the customer of $15,100/year from costs now incurred by buying at existing crash-impact specifications. Insert this number under the "clearly superior" rating in column 4.

Obviously, the customer may dispute either the assessments of his cost or the assessment of our cost-effectiveness, or both. But this example is intended only as a cost-justifying illustration.

• Example 3 describes a computerized planning and distribution system, coupled to capabilities for minor assembly. We believe that with terminals in the customer facilities tied in to our mainframe computer, we can reduce order-placement costs by 25 percent. Currently, the customer processes 500 purchase orders a month. At an average cost of $20/order (no fixed overheads included), this amounts to $10,000/mo. A 25 percent reduction in these costs is $2,500.

By meshing our delivery with customer requirements on a daily basis for 90 percent of his requirements, and every three days for the remaining 10 percent, we can reduce his inventories. The average inventory on the items we supply is $75,000. At an annual carrying cost of 30 percent, this would be a reduction of inventory by $22,500 and a savings in carrying cost of $1,875.

By picking and packing parts into kits ready for assembly, we reduce handling and assembly time by 8 percent. Handling and assembly costs are now estimated at $425,000/yr., or approximately $35,000/mo. An 8 percent reduction in these costs is $2,833.

The total of these cost items is $7,708/mo. or $92,496/yr. Insert these numbers under the appropriate column headings.

Bottom Line Assessment

Value selling justifies the sale competitively by demonstrating:

• How customer requirements—both specified and implied— are satisfied
• How customer requirements are satisfied at least total cost in use

Chapter 6

THE VALUE SELLING PRESENTATION

The Value Selling Presentation implements the rationale of the Value Selling Checklist (see Table 5-1). What the salesperson has assessed in terms of (1) the customer's requirements and (2) the customer's appraisal of his and his competitor's value contribution toward the satisfaction of those requirements become the foundation for the sales presentation. Hence, it is critical that we understand thoroughly the premises upon which the value selling concept is built.

Premise 1: Value as Acknowledged or Perceived by Customer

The notion of value is not intrinsic to the seller's product or service offering. It is acknowledged or perceived by the customer. It entails two dimensions, both of which are basic:

1. The satisfaction of purchase requirements as the customer defines or specifies them
2. Cost-effectiveness, that is, the total cost to the customer at which that satisfaction is realized

Premise 2: Purchase Requirements as Derived Requirements

Customer purchase requirements are derived requirements. They flow from or are driven by demands imposed upon the customer by three factors:

1. *Product-imposed demands*—Those set in motion by the customer's product or service itself. These demands are for performance; reliability; maintainability; ease of operation; appearance; conformity with government, professional, insurance, or industry standards; and protection of proprietary rights.

2. *Process-imposed demands*—Those that engineering, manufacturing, distribution, financial, and administrative processes create. They are for additional capacity; improved quality; increased efficiency; reduced operating cost; elimination or reduction of waste or hazardous materials; improvement of physical environment; and conformance with government, industry, or professional standards for health and safety.

3. *Market- and competition-imposed demands*—Those that the market and competition compel the customer to address. They include improved quality of product or service offerings; improved delivery or time performance; reduced prices; increased or improved service and support of product; broader, more diversified, or more specialized product mix; more favorable terms and conditions of sale; and more favorable terms of payment.

Premise 3: Demands Interpreted as Requirements

The three demands of Premise 2 are identified and interpreted as "requirements" by buying influences. They are identified by the customer's technical, operating, and management people who define the product, process, or market and competition demands in terms of purchase requirements. The demands are then translated into purchase specifications by specifiers, users, and staff or functional managers so that the purchase may actually proceed. Purchase specifications are written in terms of work descriptions, product design and performance characteristics, physical features or properties of materials, and parts and components. They are further defined by quantity, time, and service support. Requirements are expressly defined by specification. They are also implied in the specification. Implied requirements are for capabilities—technical, production, financial, and management.

Premise 4: Perceptions of Value as Differing According to Buying Influences

Buying influences have different perceptions of value. Where price may be a primary value contribution to the financial manager, it may be of little importance to a design engineer. Where assured reliability of quality may be critical to the design engineer, it may be ignored or assumed by the purchasing agent. Value perceptions tend to reflect specialized business or functional interests and the bases on which they are measured. What serves a buying influence's interests or affects his performance rating becomes a prime factor in his value perceptions.

Premise 5: The Common Element of Cost

Despite the differences in perception, there is one common element that transcends all perceptions of value. And that element is cost. Every purchase entails cost, not only the price itself, but also the costs that are subsequent to the purchase. Therefore, cost to the customer is a basic dimension of value for the customer.

The Value Selling Presentation shown in Figure 6-1 translates product/service features and seller capabilities into terms that relate to customer-specified and -implied requirements. It shows the meshing of customer requirements and supplier product/ service features and capabilities with cost-effectiveness (cost re- duction, cost avoidance, cost offsets). The more direct the rela- tionship of feature and capability to specific requirement, the more effective is the presentation. The more that relationship is supported and reinforced in terms of cost saving, cost avoidance, or cost offsets, the more effective is the presentation. Hence, the thrust of the sales presentation is twofold: (1) to mesh directly product features and sales capabilities to requirements, and (2) to dem- onstrate cost-effectiveness to the customer in that meshing.

Figure 6–1. Objective of the value selling presentation.

A = Customer Requirements
B = Supplier Product/Service
        Features and Capabilities
C = Cost-Effectiveness

A B

No Meshing

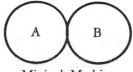

Mininal Meshing

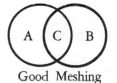

Good Meshing

Ideal Meshing

Preparing the Value Selling Presentation

Here it is important to reiterate a point that has been made several times before. In industrial and institutional markets, the "customer" is rarely an individual. The customer is a network of buying influences whose judgments and decisions collectively determine a yes or no to the sale. The larger the organization and the more complex and long-term the consequences of the purchase, the more numerous and functionally diverse those buying influences will be. Hence, the Value Selling Presentation must be specifically tailored to the interests and motivations of each specific buying influence. The rationale for the value-selling presentation is the same: to mesh offerings with requirements cost-effectively. But its orientation, its relationship of features and capabilities to requirements, and its relationship of customer cost to value will differ depending on the buying influence involved. What that presentation must say to the product designer (a specifier) may be of little importance to the production manager (a user). And what may be of critical importance to the controller (higher management) may be poorly understood or not even recognized by the purchasing agent (a buying influence by definition).

> EXAMPLE 1: The unique magazine that permits the packaging of more powerful microelectronics devices and circuitry may be an interesting feature of your product to the financial manager whose opinion may have a bearing on the source the customer selects. It is a critical feature to the design engineer, however, if the customer's market and product demands are for miniaturization without loss of performance or effectiveness. It also could be of more than passing interest to the production manager, who because of the magazine's design will have fewer components to assemble and smaller inventories to maintain. If the sales presentation can now mesh this feature with the customer's requirements and emphasize the added dimension of cost-effectiveness, the task of value selling is complete. Fewer components, faster assembly time, and lower inventories translate into cost savings and cost avoidance. Quantifying those savings then becomes a matter of probing to learn actual cost experience, or estimating those costs as best you can.

EXAMPLE 2: Your trucks may have the most effective on-board vehicle monitoring system for capturing road and mileage data and transferring it to a mainframe computer for analysis. In and of itself, that feature may be of moderate interest to the purchasing agent who has other trucks and sources that are "approved" for the customer's application. However, it is of vital importance to the traffic manager. or distribution manager who is charged with controlling fleet operating costs. If the sales presentation can demonstrate that feedback from truck to computer can show where and how fuel can be saved, engine life extended, and vehicle dispatching, routing, and utilization improved, the task of value selling is well on the way to being realized. Quantifying those cost benefits is all that remains. And that may be merely a matter of comparing "before and after" costs per mile, per hour, per vehicle, using actual or estimated rates to make the calculation.

EXAMPLE 3: It may be of no particular interest to the customer's operations manager that you have banking offices in every major commercial center in this country and abroad. After all, that claim can be made by dozens of other institutions. However, the fact that those offices are staffed with professionals who specialize in hedging, cross-currency arbitrage, domestic and international treasury management, as well as conventional banking and banking services may be of major concern to the vice-president of Finance. Charged with shifting funds from one location to another and protecting the company's assets from dilution through currency fluctuations, he can easily relate your service features and capabilities to his company's financial management needs. And he can probably supply the numbers that allow you to quantify those benefits in terms of cost savings, cost avoidance, and cost offsets.

To be effective, the Value Selling Presentation must do the following:

Identify and be responsive to the customer's requirements as they are defined or specified by buying influences. In some cases requirements may not be described by formal specification. And in a few cases, they may not even be acknowledged. But the Value Selling Presentation must proceed from a recognition of customer requirements as they are perceived or might be perceived by relevant buying influences.

Demonstrate how product and service features satisfy expressly defined requirements. Where appropriate, it must demonstrate how supplier capabilities (technical, production, financial, and management) satisfy customer-implied requirements.

Establish cost-effectiveness to the customer. If price is not competitive because your product or service warrants a premium, the presentation must show why that premium is warranted through cost-effectiveness. The bottom-line consideration to the customer should be satisfaction of his requirements at the lowest total cost.

The following examples illustrate the application of these principles.

EXAMPLE *1:*

Dick Barrows, plant manager for Pioneer Plastics, an end user

"With 22 injection molding machines, cycling every 15 seconds, and doing it 24 hours a day, 5 days a week, any interruption in production is costly. We believe our downtime experience has been too high."

Salesperson

Addresses customer requirements— process-imposed demand for improved machine performance

"Mr. Barrows, a common cause of machine failure is the hydraulic oil used. With your machines requiring 2,000 psi and operating at 180°F, that factor can be critical. If the oil you use gums up the works, so that you have to flush out the system, tear down units, and clean parts, that can be an expensive proposition.

Addresses product features that relate to customer requirements

"Now, in view of the pressure, temperature, and operating requirements your machines must meet, I strongly recommend our Free-Flow 32 hydraulic oils. They come in a broad range of viscosity grades, so they can be almost formulated to the unique demands of each of your molding machines. All of these oils contain a patented additive that breaks up and dissolves sludge and contaminants, and carries them out of your system into the filter.

"Our experience with the Marlow Company, which operates the same machines as Pioneer, should be of interest to you. Before Marlow switched to Free-Flow 32 it had all kinds of problems. At least twice a month it would have to shut down a machine, flush out old oil and sludge, clean parts, and lubricate. Since they switched, they have not had a single pump failure, and have not had to change the oil on any machine for over a year and a half. And that is the typical example.

Addresses cost-effectiveness—cost savings, and cost avoidance

"Now, I don't know exactly what it costs you to operate your machines, but I do know the savings realized at Pioneer. They totaled well over $2,000 a machine for the 12-month period they documented. This covered savings in costs of lost production, actual tear-down and repair time, start-up, and lubrication. I would be willing to bet that if you took the past year's pump failure rate on your twenty-two machines and considered the same kinds of cost, you'd be talking at least $50,000 to $60,000. If switching to Free-Flow 32 makes for only a 75 percent improvement from your current failure rate—and I'm certain it can do better—we're looking at $35,000 to $45,000 of savings and cost avoidance."

EXAMPLE *2:*

Charlie Cole, materials manager for Specialty Products, an end-user customer

"It's almost a joke when people around here talk about 'planning'. We're so shorthanded that we're constantly chasing our tail. We process hundreds of requisitions each month, and in 80 percent of the cases they're for small-quantity, low-value items, which will be requisitioned again the next month."

Salesperson

"I truly appreciate your problem, Mr. Cole, and I believe we can help you. In reviewing our business with you over the past 12 months we have found that you placed 375 purchase orders in total, for an average of 35 orders per month. The number of line items per order ranged from a single item to as many as 42. Prices were $0.69 to $23.75 per unit and total expenditures for the year amounted to $43,000. Although we appreciate your business, the way you've been buying works neither to your nor our advantage. Just as frequent small orders are inefficient to buy, they're inefficient to supply. And I know we're only supplying part of your mechanical MRO requirements.

"Bluestone products carries the most complete line of mechanical maintenance, repair, and operating items in the tri-state area. All told we stock over 200,000 separate and distinct line items. To my knowledge, there is not an item you buy that we cannot supply. Within the past year we have automated our warehousing, material handling, and picking and packing operations. We have computerized our order-entry system to give customers instant and economical access to our entire inventory. Under our Minuteman supply program we ensure our customers of delivery within 24 hours of order placement on 80 percent of the items in our inventory.

Addresses customer requirements— process-imposed demand for increased efficiency

Addresses service features that relate to customer requirements

On 15 percent of the balance of those items we ensure delivery within 48 hours, and on the remaining 5 percent, delivery within 72 hours. Orders need not go through the formal purchasing procedure. They can be placed directly by plant operating people, designated by Purchasing, and for amounts approved by Purchasing. Monthly, we will provide a detailed report on orders placed, line item by line item, unit prices and extended dollars, by authorized individual or department. Quarterly and annually, we will supply cumulative data in the same format.

"Unfortunately, the costs of buying and holding materials are not always recognized. But I'm sure from what you say about being understaffed and chasing your tail, Mr. Cole, that you do. Now, if you can get 50 percent of your mechanical MRO items under our Minuteman program—that's twice what we're supplying now—let's just estimate what that would do to reduce or avoid costs. Here is a little worksheet I've put together for making the calculations.

Costs of Buying and Holding Materials	At the Current Rate of 35 Orders/Month, for Approximately 25% of Requirements	Under the Minuteman Program, for 50% of Requirements
Cost of requisitioning	(you fill in)	0
Cost of purchase orders		0
Cost of receiving		0
Cost of storage and handling		0

Continued

Costs of Buying and Holding Materials	At the Current Rate of 35 Orders/Month, for Approximately 25% of Requirements	Under the Minuteman Program, for 50% of Requirements
Interest on capital invested		0
Taxes		0
Insurance		0
Excess and obsolescence		0

"By buying under our Minuteman program, Mr. Cole, you can save 30-40 percent of the costs you're now incurring to buy and hold those MRO materials. And you'll free up your buyers and yourself from the unnecessary time and effort now expended in chasing paper. I know you can spend it more productively elsewhere."

EXAMPLE *3:*

Arnold Meyer, financial vice-president, S&H Distributors, an end user

"I understand you've been talking to Joe Kuchinski, our manager of distribution about selling us cars and trucks we plan to buy to handle our increased business volume. You'd better have a good story, because money around here is tight, and we figure we can do better by leasing than by buying."

Salesperson

Addresses customer requirements— acknowledged: process-imposed demand for

"At first glance, it may appear that leasing is less expensive but let's explore the facts more closely. Joe tells me you're considering a fleet of six Buick Rivieras, two Oldsmobile Front Drive 98s, two Dodge Mini-Ram vans, and two Ford Ranger pickups. We can

*additional
vehicles;
unacknowledged;
implied
requirements for
services to
support
acknowledged
demand*

supply all of those vehicles fully equipped with automatic transmission, air conditioning, power steering and brakes, AM radio, rear window defrost, tinted glass, radial tires and base engine; and we can provide immediate delivery on all of them.

"But you know, Mr. Meyer, you're not only buying or leasing a car or truck. Your requirements are for safe and reliable transportation, so service considerations should not be overlooked. We are five minutes from your warehouse, and we have a highly qual-

*Addresses
product and
service features
that relate to
customer
requirements*

ified staff of service mechanics and technicians. We have the most up-to-date facilities and diagnostic equipment, as well as a complete stock of spare and replacement parts.

"But let me get back to the matter of leasing or buying. If you had a 24-month, 60,000-mile open-end lease—which is common for a fleet of your size—you would pay $90,500 total for the use of the twelve vehicles. That works out to $3,771 per month. Using a monthly depreciation rate of 2.5 percent, each vehicle would have to be worth at least 40 percent of the original value at the end of the lease period. Under the open-end contract, you the customer would be liable for any difference in that value. And that's an important risk you should consider. If you buy these vehicles from us, I'm sure we can work out a price for all vehicles at around $138,000 to $140,000. Assuming you use them over the same 24-month period, their trade-in value, on average, will be 50 percent

*Addresses cost-
effectiveness—
cost savings*

of the original price, so the actual investment works out to one-half of $138,000, or $69,000. That's a saving of more than $20,000—$90,500 less $69,000—$90,000—over what you'd pay if you leased. If you chose to sell the vehicles to your employees, you'd get even better than the 50 percent trade-in value. Further, by buying you don't have to worry about mileage limits or surcharges. And, you get topnotch service as an added plus."

EXAMPLE **4:**

Carla Shoup, packaging engineer, Cosmos Electronics, an OEM

"The constant handling and movement of our products during shipment from plant to customer results in an unacceptable rate of breakage and damage. Our products are delicate. They are telecommunications and instrumentation devices and they're extremely sensitive."

Salesperson

Addresses customer requirements— market-imposed demand for delivery of acceptable product through improved packaging

"Ms. Shoup, Dower Chemicals has just introduced a new molded foam called Mat-Tech that is the answer to protection of products that are fragile and high in value.

"Mat-Tech is a styrene polymer-based material that produces resilient foam of uniform consistency. It provides multiple-impact cushioning protection, and its consistency ensures that the cushioning characteristics will be met repeatedly and predictably. The specific properties of Mat-Tech are described in some detail on these information sheets. As you'll see they cover compression creep at various psi loadings, compressive strength, tensile

Addresses product features that relate to

*customer
requirements*

*Addresses cost-
effectiveness—
cost savings and
cost avoidance*

strength, thermal conductivity, water
absorption, and water vapor perma-
nence. I believe you'll find the numbers
quite impressive.

"Mat-Tech can be used with conventional molding technology, and both
mold design and construction are the
same as with EPS resins. Mat-Tech
requires no special handling and storage measures, such as refrigeration or
venting of volatile vapors, so there are
no unpleasant surprises when you
specify our product. As a matter of fact,
Mat-Tech reduces cost because pack-
ers do not have to be specially trained
to use it, and less skilled people can
be employed in the molding process.
This is because the product is so consistent that critical judgment is not required as it is with other molding materials. Further, because of its
consistent compressive strength, Mat-
Tech resists deformation of compressive creep at loadings. This means that
molded parts retain their original shape
and properties with no loss, thereby
reducing scrappage and deviation from
specs. Experience at other electronics
manufacturers has shown 20 to 25 percent savings on this element alone. But
the real savings are those that result
from less breakage and damage of
shipped goods. If you obtained only a
10 percent improvement through the
use of Mat-Tech—and I think that's
extremely conservative—what do you
think that would amount to?"

EXAMPLE **5:**

*Jerry Callahan, purchasing agent,
Thornwood Manufacturing, an OEM*

"It has been our practice to maintain four or five sources and, frankly,

unless you can come up with substantial price concessions, I don't see any reason for changing that practice. Certainly not in today's unpredictable market."

Salesperson

"Mr. Callahan, price is an important consideration, and Smith and Lockwood has always met competitive prices. Where necessary we've even bettered them. But when you buy as many items as Thornwood does as frequently as it does, price per item or purchase is really not that important. The critical consideration should be the total cost of delivered product, as and when you need it, for all items over the total contract or agreement time. And on that score I believe we do considerably better than most of our competitors.

Addresses customer requirements— market-imposed demand for lower price

"Five years ago, Smith and Lockwood made a commitment to becoming a major supplier in the steel service and supply business. We made substantial investments in the most up-to-date and automated forming and fabrication equipment. We entered into long-term agreements with the most efficient mills both here and abroad, so we're able to get metal at the quality we specify, exactly when we need it. Those agreements assure us of steel better than if we had our own mills, so even if demand goes up we'll still be able to supply. We maintain one of the largest inventories in the business— over 500 million pounds in all shapes, forms, and sizes, including specialty items like prefinished steel and special alloy metals. And we maintain them at service centers that are all within 2 to

Addresses product and service features that relate to customer requirements

6 hours' driving time of your plants. Now that surely has to be worth something to Thornwood.

"Over the past 12 months we supplied $223,000 of bar, sheet, rod, and tube in both carbon and stainless. We've analyzed the data and developed a detailed profile of what you've bought from us by grade, size, and width, as well as by any special characteristics you specified. On standard items that we've supplied to you before, our delivery was within 24 to 48 hours of order placement. On items we had not supplied before but which are still standard, we delivered in 75 percent of the cases in less than our normal lead time. On special items, we came within a fraction of meeting your specified delivery 100 percent of the time. But in over 40 percent of those purchases you specified delivery in less than our quoted lead times. And the only reason we delivered as well as we did was because Jim Malloy, the technical specialist we assigned to Thornwood, works so well with your Engineering people. Together they were able to get specifications finalized and passed on for processing in short order. And when we couldn't supply from the service center nearest to you, we shipped it from another. Or if it called for special processing, we got our order in quickly with the mill best able to handle it.

"Mr. Callahan, I think you'll agree that this has provided substantial value benefits to Thornwood. Delivery within 24 to 48 hours of order placement eliminates inventory and ensures supply only as needed. Delivery in less than our normal lead time reduces the inventory required over normal replace-

Addresses cost-effectiveness—cost savings and cost avoidance

ment time and eliminates all safety stock required by late delivery. With interest on working capital at 12 to 15 percent a year, those savings in inventory should be considerable. And for a larger share of Thornwood's business, they could be even greater.

"As for Jim Malloy, I'm sure you'll agree his acceptance by your Engineering people has more than paid off. It's saved not only Engineering man-hours, but also direct product cost. Do you remember the motor screen on your K-305 blower? You were making it out of expanded metal with 40 spot welds for about 6 bucks a unit. Malloy recommended that you stamp it out of perforated metal and you saved about $4.75 a unit. Now that's got to be worth something."

Now that you have read these five examples of value selling presentations, try your hand at developing a value selling presentation for your own product or service.

1. Identify clearly and completely the customer's requirements. Remember, those that are specified or expressly defined get prime attention. But remember, too, that the customer's requirements may also be implied by what he specifies. Delivery of product demands production or supply capability. Assurance of quality demands engineering and process controls. The customer either may not always acknowledge these implied requirements or may assume that they can be satisfied equally by all suppliers. If you think they are important considerations, identify and address them.

Again, remember that the customer's requirement is typically a derived one, imposed by the demands of his product, his process, or his market and competition. Depending on who the buying influence is who now speaks as the "customer," assess his perceptions of those imposed demands. Those perceptions could color his view of what his requirements truly are.

_____

_____

_____

_____

_____

2. List all those product and service features your offering provides that relate to the customer's specified and implied requirements. The more direct the relation of a feature to the satisfaction of the requirement, the more effective it will be. Features ought not be simply stated. They should be described so that they serve a purpose or perform a function that the requirement calls for. Product or service features do something, accomplish something that the requirement demands. They prevent corrosion, activate a power supply, improve fuel consumption, or monitor and manage contractor performance.

_____

_____

_____

_____

_____

3. Think cost—cost savings, cost avoidance, cost offsets that result from increased income or improved cash flow. In satisfying the customer's requirements, how do your product or service features result in cost-effectiveness? To help you think along these lines, go back and review Chapter 3. Remember, cost is not always as it's accounted for. Cost is any expenditure of time, material, or other resources. Don't be intimidated by the notion of it, or get hung up by the thought that you can't come up with "real" or "actual" costs in dollar-and-cents terms. The most important thing to accomplish is to establish the relationship between your product or service feature and the fact that labor time is saved, idle machine time is avoided, scrap losses are

reduced, revenue flow is speeded up, or income is increased to offset or absorb more favorably overheads and other indirect expenses. Once the relationship is established by example, by illustration, by analogy, the quantifying of that relationship becomes a less fearsome task. We can estimate cost-effectiveness. We can bracket and interpolate possible cost consequences. What is the maximum amount that could be saved, avoided, offset? What is the minimum? What is a likely amount?

It is common for advertising copy and sales presentations to talk about how a seller's offering will improve the customer's "profit." I strongly discourage this practice. The relationship between actually incurred cost and profit is at best shaky and uncertain, even under the most sophisticated accounting systems. Profit is the net result of all incomes less all costs and expenses. And to suggest that any specific product or service feature will result in additional profit is to invite debate, if not ridicule. You are on safer and stronger ground when you think "cost."

_____

_____

_____

_____

_____

Chapter 7

HANDLING OBJECTIONS, COMPLAINTS, AND CHANGES

If the Value Selling Presentation discussed in Chapter 6 is well prepared, you will be able to anticipate objections and deal with them before they come up. But even with the best presentation, you cannot anticipate all objections, particularly those that are really excuses, alibis, or personal rationalizations for avoiding a buying decision. And this possibility is always there as long as the personal factor is present in the buying process.

But where an objection is not a delaying tactic or an out-and-out evasion, you should view it as an opportunity in disguise. The customer who raises an objection is not saying, "I will not buy." He is expressing doubt or disagreement. He is saying, "I'm not convinced" or, "You have not provided sufficient information or evidence to make me comfortable with a buying decision."He is looking for a resolution of those doubts or disagreements. He is looking for reassurance. Indeed, when selling to prospective customers, the best prospects are the ones who raise objections.

Complaints are "grievances or expressions of dissatisfaction by the customer." They arise because of misunderstandings, erroneous or incomplete information, real or imagined failures by the seller to do or supply what the customer expected. Like objections, complaints to the value seller can also be opportunities in disguise. If properly handled, they can provide the basis for improving goodwill, even generating additional business.

Years ago, I heard a talk by a senior executive from a major *Fortune* 500 company that confirmed this very point. He said that when price, quality, and delivery are equal, the pendulum usually swings to the supplier giving the best service, not necessarily on this one transaction but including past service factors. One of these factors is how does it handle complaints? Does it take a defensive attitude immediately, or does it say the customer is always right? Either is equally wrong. His company preferred that a qualified representative thoroughly investigate the complaint and report facts. He would rather be told and proved wrong so he could correct the cause of the complaint than be agreed with and have the same failure reoccur.

Customer-initiated changes are, in one important respect, like objections and complaints. They demand an appropriate response. In industrial and institutional markets, changes are common and to be expected. They arise from the fact that the customer's requirements are derived, so when changes alter those requirements, they force changes in purchases. For example: A change in the customer's product design may necessitate a change in materials or component design. A change in a customer's process may require a change in equipment performance or specification. A change in the customer's market or competitive position may compel a change in supply quantities or delivery rates.

Changes can be requested by the customer or they can be directed by the customer when he buys to his own specifications. In either event, changes affect the technical, production, or management considerations made by the seller at the time of the original sale. They can affect utilization of resources, schedules, and time. They can affect the ability to satisfy other customer business. In many instances they can adversely affect cost. And in some instances they can adversely affect profit. Accordingly, changes can be rejected, resisted, or complied with, but they cannot be easily ignored. And for this reason, changes can become to the value seller another opportunity in disguise.

What turns objections, complaints, and changes into opportunities is that they provide another opening for value selling. They provide you with another chance to relate product and service features to customers' requirements. They provide the salesperson with another chance to demonstrate cost-effectiveness. To illustrate:

When the customer raises an objection during the sales presentation, he identifies a clear and specific target for you to address. Is the objection "The price is too high"? You can now demonstrate and prove lower total cost. Is the objection "Your product won't do the job"? You can now review customer requirements—the implied as well as specified ones—and show how product and service features do relate to requirements and do in fact satisfy them.

When you can successfully answer a customer objection, you're in a favorable position to close the sale.

When the customer levels a complaint, with or without justification, he expects an explanation. He expects a review and report of the pertinent facts and circumstances involved. He also expects proposed solutions to the problem generated.

- The review of facts may show that the complaint is unwarranted. The customer's information may be incorrect, or the conclusions he's drawn from the information he has may be incorrect.
- The review of circumstances may show that the cause of the complaint was not your doing; it resulted from other factors, such as incomplete specifications, faulty drawings, or customer action or failure to act. If this is the case, you can now restate and reinforce the value selling message. You can re-relate product and service features to customer requirements. You can reestablish cost-effectiveness.
- In proposing a solution to the problem generated, you have the opportunity to "sell up." You can show how the problem, or problems, cited call for additional product features or supplier

capabilities not recognized by the customer initially. You can demonstrate how your product and service features, together with your organization's capabilities, satisfy these newly recognized requirements. You can establish cost-effectiveness to support the acceptance of the enhanced proposal.

Handling Objections

Probably the most difficult prospect to sell is the one who remains silent or provides little feedback during the sales presentation. Perhaps he does so to appear strong and immovable. Or perhaps he is unsure of himself and is fearful of displaying openly his lack of knowledge or expertise. Regardless of why he is silent, if the prospect has doubts or concerns that are unresolved, the sale is in jeopardy. For this reason, it is important that in preparing your value selling presentation you anticipate as many objections as possible. By mentally putting yourself in the prospect's shoes, you can focus on those objections or concerns the prospect is likely to have in mind. If he raises them, you are prepared. If he is silent, or doesn't raise them, you know they must be addressed and resolved before you can consider the presentation complete.

But remember, the "prospect" is but one customer buying influence, and his perceptions of value may not be the same as those of other buying influences with different functions or responsibilities. What may be a doubt or fear to a product designer may be of little concern to a purchasing agent. What may be an area of disagreement to the finance manager may be thoroughly acceptable to the manager of production. So in anticipating objections, know the buying influence who now speaks as the "customer." What does he do? What is he accountable for? Knowing where he's coming from will make you better able to tailor an effective response to the objections he raises as well as the ones he has but doesn't raise.

The customer—that is, the buying influence—can raise objections on any matter he disagrees with, or on any point that is unclear. If he disagrees, he wants to be shown why he should not. If he wants clarification, he seeks more information. If he has doubts, he wants to be reassured. To the inexperienced salesperson, objections may be negative factors to the sale, and something to be avoided. Skilled and experienced salespeople know differently. They welcome and invite objections. Objections, effectively answered, are links in the chain that holds the sales presentation together.

At times, an objection may seem petty or irrelevant. Indeed, an objection may be raised as a diversionary or delaying tactic. This is not an uncommon practice in industrial sales situations when your presentation may be made to a group. This kind of objection usually occurs for either of the following reasons:

1. To demonstrate importance or knowledge; to show the others that the person raising the objection is a factor to be reckoned with
2. As a delaying tactic, or to throw a roadblock in the way of a disapproved of sale

For these reasons, I strongly advise you never to ignore an objection, no matter how minor or trivial it may seem. And this is particularly so when the presentation is before a group or committee. Remember, the customer is a network of buying influences, and although there may be only one person who can say yes, there are others who can say no. To ignore the diversionary or delaying objective is to invite a no from the objector. He says no either to protect his ego or to kill the sale he didn't want in the first place.

This advice is contrary to what appears in much sales training literature. Salespeople are often instructed to ignore the objection and to proceed with the presentation as if the objection had never been raised. Or they are instructed to say, "I'll get to that later" with no intention of ever doing so.

This tactic of handling objections may be effective in consumer sales, where the customer is an individual. By dramatizing product features, by playing on the emotional or psychological factors that motivate the customer, the presentation may blur or eradicate the objection. This can easily happen if the objection is minor. It is less likely to happen, even in consumer sales, when the objection is major. And in industrial markets, because the customer is not an individual reacting like a personal computer, all objections should be considered important enough to answer.

Techniques for Handling Objections

I have said that objections are opportunities in disguise. If you answer them effectively, you are now in a strong position to ask for the order. Clearly, if the objection as stated is the customer's only concern, there is nothing in the way of closing the sale. Indeed, one of the best times to attempt the close is after an objection is answered successfully—if for no other reason than that you should be thoroughly familiar with objection-handling techniques.

Objection-handling techniques also serve another important purpose: They provide a bridge from one point in a sales presentation to another. When the customer raises a doubt or objection, he introduces a gap or fault in the continuity of the sales presentation. You must bridge that gap or fault so that you can proceed with the original plan. It is essential that you don't become sidetracked or diverted by the objection, something that can easily happen when a salesperson loses sight of the overall presentation strategy. The concept that underlies that strategy is value selling. And any technique you use to handle an objection must allow you to bridge the gap smoothly and return to the value selling message. Indeed, the more you incorporate the value selling message into the answer to the objection, the more effective that answer becomes.

Following are tried and proved techniques that value sellers can use to handle customer objections successfully:

1. **Meet the objection head on and answer it directly.** This technique addresses the objection and refutes it point by point. The effectiveness of the technique depends in large measure on your skill and tact. It is more confrontational than other techniques, and can easily lead to arguments. There are situations, however, when it cannot be avoided. In those situations remember that how you say it may be more crucial that what you say. Smile when you say it.

EXAMPLE: You know, Ms. Robbins, I'm afraid I have to take issue with you. Not every supplier provides the same assurance of quality as we do. Vector Manufacturing is the only supplier that provides you with not only a full warranty on new transformers but also a new product warranty on every replacement part or service repair. But most important, we make our products right the first time; just consider the following: . . .

Go back to your value selling presentation.

2. **Evade the objection with a "yes but. . . ."** Here, treat the objection as a misconception. Don't tell the customer he's wrong, but show why the objection does not apply, or why the doubt is unwarranted. Evading an objection is neither ignoring it nor meeting it head on. It is something in between. If properly used, it provides an excellent bridge for proceeding with your presentation. There are also times when it will provide a good opportunity for closing.

EXAMPLE: Yes, Mr. Morris, our rates are not low. But when you think of the cost of moving merchandise from suppliers to you, and from you to your distributors, the total cost is very low. And that's what really counts, isn't it? Capital Carriers is one of the few companies capable of putting together all transportation services—air, rail, truck, warehousing, and traffic management—into a single package. This helps you to increase sales, reduce damaged and lost shipments, and cut costs by 5 to 25 percent. Let me show you in more detail how we can do this. . . .

Go back into the value selling presentation.

EXAMPLE: Yes, Mr. Matsushima, I know we're not a household name in the telecommunications industry. But Bellwood Cables meets each and every one of your specification requirements. It meets your demand for strength, frequency, resistance, and operating temperatures. And it meets them with a comfortable margin of safety. On top of that, its low weight and diameter will reduce the costs of materials and assembly time for your new product applications. Just consider the high-frequency characteristics and mechanical toughness of our 6732 cable, which we've recommended for the Project Daphne System.

Go back into the value selling presentation.
There are variations of the "yes but. . . ." technique. They all are designed to evade the customer-raised objections, that is, to avoid

answering them head on. They all entail some appropriate phrasing to bridge the gap between the presentation before the objection and after it. Following are a few examples:

"That raises an interesting question, but. . . ."
"That's an interesting observation, but. . . ."
"I really can't dispute the point, but. . . ."
"Obviously, anything is possible, but. . . ."
"You may have a point, but. . . ."

3. **Analyze the problem.** This is a technique for directing the thrust of the objection by drawing the customer into the process of resolving his own doubts or fears. By analyzing and uncovering specific points of concern, you can now address them and guide the customer to resolve them himself.

> EXAMPLE: Now let's look at that a little bit more closely, Ms. Rosario. You suggested it might be better to go with a large national accounting firm, rather than a smaller one. But really, is it the size of the firm that's important, or is it the caliber of the people who are assigned to your account? Is it the fact that your accountants operate nationally, or is it more important that you get reports, information, and professional advice when you want it? For example. . . .

Go back into your value selling presentation.

4. **Question the objection.** Like the "analyze the problem" approach, this technique is designed to gain more information. It does so by asking the customer to explain why he thinks the way he does. Why does he disagree? Why does he have the doubts or concerns he does? The effectiveness of this technique depends in large measure on how the question is posed. If it is posed aggressively or antagonistically, it can easily generate a similar type of response. In that event, rather than eliciting information, the question evokes antagonism. The question should be asked in low key, and to be more productive it should be open-ended. This means it requires something more than a yes or no answer.

> EXAMPLE: In view of the critical nature of your application, Dr. Frankel, you're certainly wise to explore all possibilities. But can

you be a little bit more specific as to what in particular concerns you about the design we've proposed?

Go back to your value selling presentation.

EXAMPLE: Our Easy-Toil cleaning compounds have been around for years, Ms. Shaeffer. So can you tell me why you think your maintenance people would have any objection to their being used here at Reliable Products?

Go back to your presentation.

5. **Capitalize on the objection.** To capitalize on the objection is to use it to your advantage. You respond to the objection in such a way that you actually reinforce the sales message. You make the sales presentation stronger than it would have been had the objection not been raised.

EXAMPLE: That's exactly the point, Ms. Lippmann; simply having features like conference calling or memory dialing is not enough. A lot of systems around already do that. What's important is that your key phone system be reliable, that it give you ensured services around the clock, seven days a week, fifty-two weeks out of the year. What's important is that it be simple to operate, easy and inexpensive to maintain. What's important is that it be flexible to meet the different demands of your different operations, and yet be capable of growing as you grow. And last but not least, what's important is that your system be backed by a company you can depend on. With all the johnny-come-latelies around, I'm sure you will agree that's an important consideration. To show you what I mean, let's consider the modular design and construction of our Aries System.

Go back into value selling.

EXAMPLE: You know, Mr. Halpern, you've actually answered your own question. Not only can you afford Stan-Mar Cabinets, you really can't afford not having them. You've already said that cost control is a major company concern. Well, let's look at the facts. Stan-Mar Cabinets take up 50 percent less space than comparable shelving. I've calculated that you've got metal bins occupying slightly more than 730 square feet of factory and warehouse space.

Our cabinets will cut that down by half and free up space for more profitable use. In terms of operating and maintenance costs, there's no comparison. You can pick or retrieve 100 percent faster from our cabinets than you can from metal shelving. Have you ever tried reaching to the top of a shaky storage bin for an envelope-sized box of 3/4-inch screws that are jammed in a back corner? Well, it's time-consuming and even dangerous. Taking them out of a cabinet drawer is a snap. And when you consider the comparative costs of installation and replacement, the difference in cost becomes even more obvious. Look at these numbers I've worked up. . . .

Go back to your value selling presentation.

An effective opening for implementing the "capitalize on the objection" technique is "I'm glad you raised that question." Whether you are in fact glad or not is really not the point. But this phrase allows you to exploit the objection and turn it to your advantage.

EXAMPLE: I'm glad you raised that question, Mr. Zopolsky. I know that any large insurance company can easily get the reputation for being cold and calculating, if not totally unconcerned with its clients' needs. But I believe that we at Springfield Mutual in no way fit that mold.

Let me relate a story to you to illustrate that point. On the twenty-third of last December, a request came into our office to prepare an actuarial study on the pros and cons of increasing contributions to a client's employee profit-sharing program. And to make matters worse, the study had to be completed in time to increase the contributions that calendar year if the findings were favorable. That means we had eight days—not eight working days, but eight days—to get the job done. And that included Christmas and the Christmas week through New Year's Eve. The client was my account, so obviously, completing the study on time was my responsibility. Personal considerations would have to wait. But do you know, Mr. Zopolsky, we had two actuaries, three accountants, and six clerical and office staff give up their holidays to get the job done on time. And that's the kind of service you can expect when you insure through Springfield Mutual. . . .

Go back into your value selling presentation.

The Objections and Answer File

Skill in handling objections comes with practice and experience. The more familiar you become with specific objections, the more able you are to respond effectively. One approach you should consider is to develop and maintain a personal file of objections and answers. Such a file identifies and records the following information situation by situation and indicates success or failure on each.

1. The objection as the customer stated it. For example, "Your price is not competitive." "We're already carrying too many lines." "We already have a supplier."

2. The buying influence who raised the objection and what his objection implied. For example:

- *Buying influence*—the plant manager.
- *Implication of the objection*—concern that production will be interrupted or slowed by delivery delays or by supplier short shipments.

- *Buying influence*—the design engineer.
- *Implication of the objection*—fear that supplier quality failure might jeopardize design integrity or product performance.

- *Buying influence*—the controller.
- *Implication of the objection*—doubt that the proposed sale is a solid investment or a wise expenditure of funds.

3. The objection-handling technique the situation calls for. Be sure the bridging statement is appropriate to the technique selected.

Bridging Statement	Objection-Handling Technique
"That's an interesting observation, but. . . ." (variation of "yes but. . . .")	Purpose—to evade the objection; treat it as misinformed or inapplicable.
"Why do you say that?"	Purpose—to develop more information so that you can address specific issues.

Bridging Statement	Objection-Handling Technique
"That's precisely what I'm getting at."	Purpose—to capitalize on the objection and turn it to your advantage.

Once an objection is answered successfully, you attempt to close the sale if the circumstances permit or return to your value selling presentation. The objection should be seen as nothing more than an interruption in the presentation flow. When you go back to the presentation, you go back to the same logic and rationale of the value selling message. Depending on the buying influence who now speaks as the "customer":

1. Identify customer requirements, both specifically defined ones and those that are implied.
2. Relate specific product or service features directly to requirements—first as they apply to specified requirements and then as they apply to the implied ones.
3. Establish cost-effectiveness. Demonstrate how product or service features not only satisfy customer requirements but also reduce cost, avoid cost, or offset cost through increased income or improved cash flow.

Not all expressions of resistance to the sales presentation are objections in the sense that we have defined that term earlier. There are those that are polite or devious ways of saying, "I'm not interested." When the prospect resorts to this form of resistance, he does so with the hope that the salesperson will give up his efforts and leave. In consumer markets, this subterfuge is common. Since personal needs and desires are the source of buying demand, the same emotional and psychological forces that motivate buying also motivate not buying. And the expressions of those motivations can be straightforward or devious.

Eliminating Obstacles

In industrial and institutional markets, however, resistance to the sales presentation is not usually a reflection of emotional or psychological response. More often it stems from doubt or dis-agreement. That is, it is a true objection. Or it stems from one of the following factors, which are more correctly obstacles or impediments to the sale itself than objections raised in a sales presentation.

1. **There is no identified requirement—formally specified or informally acknowledged—that the prospect recognizes.** Remember, industrial and institutional requirements are impersonal. They are derived from a customer's product, process, or market and competitive demands. If those demands are not identified or perceived, there is no requirement. Hence, to deliver a sales presentation where there is no requirement to satisfy becomes a clear invitation to resistance. The fact that the prospect has electric-fired furnaces is an obstacle to selling him gas-regulating instrumentation. The fact that the prospect is phasing out a product and replacing it with a new one is an impediment to selling him more components specifically designed for the obsolete product.

2. **The specification or description of the requirement blocks or impedes the sale.** Industrial and institutional requirements are translated into purchase specifications or work scope definitions. These are the formal descriptions or statements of particulars that suppliers must meet in order to satisfy requirements. Oftentimes, an item of purchase is "spec-controlled," which means that a particular supplier's design of that item has been incorporated into the purchase specification as the only qualified design for a product or process application. The qualification may be the result of the supplier's earlier design efforts; it may be the result of the customer's design decisions or his testing and evaluation findings.

In any event, once an item is spec-controlled there is a definite obstacle to selling that item by any supplier not qualified or so approved. Clearly, for a would-be seller to avoid resistance, he would first have to overcome the impediment of source qualification. And that would involve activities and effort well beyond the scope of the selling function alone. What the salesperson should direct his attention to under those circumstances is not the sale of the item but the sale of his company's capability to qualify. The sales presentation should be directed toward selling—that is gaining agreement on—the opportunity to qualify. Once the impediment of qualification is removed, then you can sell the product.

3. **There is no funding or appropriation to support the purchase.** The claim of no money or insufficient funds is a common excuse for not buying. And in consumer markets, salespeople are thoroughly familiar with prospects who use that claim as an alibi to avoid a buying decision. Indeed, such people are more properly referred to as "suspects" to distinguish them from true prospects, who have both the desire and means to buy. But in industrial and institutional markets, the lack of funding can be a real deterrent to a purchase; in those markets, purchases are made against budgets and funding appropriations. Budgets identify specific items of product or service to be purchased in a fiscal period, and they allot specific dollars for their purchase. Appropriations are allocations of specific dollars to specific items of purchase. They are employed for products and services not already covered under operating or other budgets.

If budgets contain no dollars to support a purchase and no special appropriation is forthcoming, no presentation, no matter how skillfully delivered, can be successful. In periods of recession or business decline, budget cutting soon becomes the general order of the day. Funds for purchase that were there before are no longer there. It may be difficult for the salesperson to accept the thought of not making a sale, but if the customer is laying off people and his executives are taking cuts in salaries you must face up to the fact that the crunch is real. Under such circumstances, the only good advice is to maintain and expand customer contacts; seek out new opportunities to sell, and wait for another day.

4. **The customer contact is not a meaningful buying influence.** One of the most common obstacles or impediments to a sale is the fact that the prospect, or more rightly, suspect has no authority to buy and no important influence to exert. In consumer sales this is sometimes a problem. But it is rarely a serious or long-lasting one. After all, if the husband is not the family manager with the power to say yes, there is always the wife. Clearly, there is only a limited number of buying influences and their spheres of interest and responsibility are not that difficult to identify and address.

But in industrial markets, particularly in large multiproduct, multilocation companies, the task of reaching a meaningful buying influence can be complex and frustrating. Titles may not mean what they seem.

- An "operations manager" in one location may have no more authority than a line foreman somewhere else. Buying influence is not necessarily commensurate with the title.

- A purchasing agent has the authority to commit, but he is usually precluded from committing once the purchase exceeds a defined dollar limit. What is that limit and who has the authority above it?
- A product engineer ordinarily has product design responsibilities. Yet at an operating plant he may have little or no influence over material or component specification. The product design function may be performed in Corporate or Division Engineering.

One of the companies I have consulted for is a technical leader for the products and applications it sells. Its salespeople are all engineers or otherwise technically trained. And their experience in the field runs from five to fifteen years. For as long as he had the account, George—let's just call him that—made call after call on a major OEM customer. This customer was already buying limited amounts of product from George's company. But for its huge size and product diversity, its purchases were negligible. George made presentations at various product manufacturing locations, and from time to time picked up additional business for prototype or limited production. The real, large-volume production business, however, continued to elude him.

As circumstances would have it, this major OEM was also a client of mine. I knew from working with the company that it had a highly decentralized purchasing function. But I also knew that they sought to improve their buying leverage by pooling or consolidating requirements. Under this scheme the purchasing manager for the largest user plant combined his quantities with those from other using locations and then bought against the total or aggregate demand. George had never called on this plant, let alone its purchasing manager. The plant was strictly a large-volume production house turning out a mature but stable product. George had always sold applications, and he sold only to engineers. Given this scenario, is it any wonder that George was not successful?

Obstacles or impediments to a sale are not always easy to distinguish from objections. The prospect (suspect) who has no budget or appropriation funds to buy may still express doubts or raise questions that suggest buying interest and intent. The prospect (suspect) who has no authority to commit or any buying influence may be reluctant to admit that fact, and instead raises "objections" like a true buying force. Meanwhile, the salesperson, anxious to close the sale, may see all resistance as objections that he must face and overcome.

The sales presentation itself, no matter how well put together, cannot overcome a true obstacle or impediment. The obstacle must be eliminated or you must expend your energy elsewhere. The effective value seller, however, can often remove the obstacle or impediment by seeking out and nullifying its basic cause. To illustrate:

• Requirements are identified by buying influences as they know or perceive product, process, and market and competitive demands. However, requirements that are real are not always seen or acknowledged. Because of inexperience, lack of information, or lack of technical or economic expertise, a buying influence may not know or understand changes in the demands that create his requirements. He may not realize that changing technology demands a change in the material he uses or the products he resells. He may not see that the changing economic climate demands a change in the quantities or volume he buys. If you can educate and convince that buying influence that such changes are imposed demands, which necessarily call for changed perceptions of requirements, the obstacle or impediment is eliminated. What was not a requirement before now is.

• When the customer's specification identifies a competitive supplier as the single approved source for what he buys, it is because that supplier has been qualified or approved for that specific purpose or application. Usually this occurs because the customer designed his product or application around that supplier's product or design. Or it is because, of all the offerings initially considered, that supplier's offering best met the customer's testing and qualification criteria. Often a supplier is the single source because the customer has expended engineering and tooling money on him and has no funds for a second source. There are several ways the value seller can eliminate this obstacle.

1. You can propose that your company perform the same tests or go through the same qualification process that the approved source went through, and provide the customer with documentation or certification for procedures and results.

2. You can propose to have your company pay an outside agency, for example, a recognized testing laboratory—to perform the necessary tests and submit findings to the customer.
3. You can propose that your company absorb the tooling or engineering costs on future sales to the customer.

In all these approaches, you may have an ally or at least an understanding listener. The customer's purchasing agent—if he is representative of his professional colleagues—is not too happy about the restrictive specification, because it restricts his ability to buy competitively. Although he cannot change the specification, he can ask that it be expanded to say "competitive supplier X or equal." This now gives him the opportunity to employ you as the "or equal," whose offerings would have to be considered unless your qualifications could be disproved. That removes the impediment and enables you to make an effective value selling presentation. Remember the following three points:

1. **Budgets are established on the basis of business plans.** They are reviewed periodically and adjusted to reflect changes in forecasts, sales, costs, or other factors. Budgets contain items of expenditure that are fixed or inflexible. They contain items that are variable in volume as well as items that are purely discretionary. Appropriations, unlike budgets, are amounts requested on an as-required basis. Such requests are reviewed, evaluated, and approved or disapproved.

2. **Budgets act as constraints on spending.** And customer budgets may not contain funds to support the purchase of what you sell. Every budget, however, constrains spending differently for specific departments, functions, or activities. A budget that imposes tight spending disciplines on one department may make it business-as-usual for another. Further, budgets are not chiseled in stone. They are changed; they are deviated from. In every organization, there is at some level an authority who can provide supplemental funding, approve a special appropriation, even juggle amounts from one budget item or department to another.

3. **Reach the higher authority and you reach a meaningful buying influence.** Reach a meaningful buying influence and you overcome the obstacle to selling.

Obstacles to a sale are not always detectable before the sales presentation. Indeed, they may unexpectedly arise during or after the presentation, even after the sale is closed. Every salesperson has experienced at one time or another one of the following situations:

- The sudden closing of a plant or operation that eliminates the need for what you sell
- A critical engineering change in the customer's product that abruptly makes the item you supply obsolete
- The loss or cancellation of customer business that makes your business superfluous

These are all real and valid impediments to a sale, and you should recognize them as such and look for new selling opportunities. More often than not, however, you can detect obstacles or impediments beforehand. To do so, you must do your homework well. You must probe, ask the right questions of the right people, and assess the answers from the only perspective that makes sense:

- Is there a requirement that needs to be satisfied?
- Are there funds available to buy?
- Who are the buying influences and can I reach them directly or through a friendly sponsor?

If the answer to any of these questions is negative, you should then ask yourself: "Can I remove or eliminate the obstacle? Can I bring to bear the necessary resources of time and people to become a qualified or approved supplier? Is there a sponsor I know, or can get to, within the customer's organization or outside of it who can help me reach a meaningful buying influence? How about the customer's architect, management consultant, banker, accounting firm?"

If after all this questioning and soul-searching you conclude that the obstacle or impediment cannot be removed, you must accept that fact and walk away. Even the best salesperson in the world can't win them all.

Handling Complaints

I defined complaints as grievances or expressions of dissatisfaction by the customer that arise from:

- Misunderstandings
- Erroneous or incomplete information
- Real or imagined failure by the seller to do or supply what the customer expected

Complaints may arise before or after the sale, but regardless of when they arise, they generate resentment and ill feelings on the part of the customer. He is distressed, disturbed, maybe downright angry. Obviously, when he is any of these, the seller-customer relation is in jeopardy.

But complaints are also opportunities. If they are properly handled they can be turned into a source of improved relations, even a source of new or expanded business. One of the most successful salespeople I know insisted that his talent for making sales was strictly a talent for solving customer problems.

In industrial markets problems are not unexpected. In fact, the larger and more complex the purchase, the more both buyer and seller expect problems to occur. Complaints arise when problems are not anticipated or when they are not addressed and satisfactorily resolved. Value sellers should look at the handling of customer complaints as first and foremost an exercise in creative problem solving.

Handling customer complaints as a problem-solving exercise involves the following three steps. All complaints require that we take the first step. If the complaint cannot be satisfied after step one, we must proceed to steps two and three.

1. **Analyze the situation; check it out and report the facts.** What is the nature of the complaint? Is it late delivery? Is it unacceptable material? Did you promise something you didn't do? Or did you do something you shouldn't have? The nature of the complaint will influence the way you handle it.

In assessing the complaint relate it to the sales situation. Does it jeopardize your sales position? Does it pose an immediate or long-term problem? Who has made the complaint? Is he or she an important buying influence? Does the complaint threaten current or future business? How the complaint relates to the sales picture is another consideration in how to handle it.

In establishing the facts, concentrate on the known ones. Differentiate between facts and opinions. A complaint that "Our records show that out of the twelve shipments you've made over the past twelve months you have been on time only seven times" is based on a statement of fact. "I don't think your delivery has been up to par" is a complaint based on opinion.

Further, in developing the facts, distinguish between relevant and irrelevant ones. Only the facts that are relevant to the complaint should be considered. If the complaint is that the item we supply fails intermittently in the customer's process, it is an irrelevant fact that it has always done that. It's irrelevant even if the customer knows it to be true. A fact that *is* relevant is that the product is supplied to the customer's performance specifications and he contributed to and also approved the design.

Often you can resolve the complaint satisfactorily merely by examining the situation and establishing the facts. This is common when the complaint is based on misinformation, incomplete, or old information. In reporting the facts or updating the data, you effectively satisfy the complaint.

> EXAMPLE: Mr. Powers, I've checked on your complaint about our holding up your assembly line because we're not delivering parts on time. The facts are these: 3,600 units were on your receiving dock April 11, the day before you called. Evidently the Receiving copies never hit your desk, or the real problem is down in Receiving. If you remember, this problem has happened before. We've been right on schedule, and you'll have all of your parts the way you ordered them. We shipped 4,500 units on April 17, the day before yesterday, and the balance of 3,600 will go out on April 29. I hope that takes care of the problem.

If the complaint cannot be resolved by correcting misinformation or reporting the facts, you must proceed to the second step.

2. **Search for possible solutions.** What will satisfy the complaint? What has worked successfully in the past? If this situation is different, what will work now?

Write down as many possible solutions as you can think of. Test them out. What is good about each? Why will it work? What is bad about each? Why won't it work?

3. **Decide on a solution or combination of solutions and propose it.** Step 2 is essentially an analytical step, a creative or brainstorming one. I've heard the phrase "imagineering," and that's a good way of describing what you do in Step 2. But Step 3 is the

decision-making step. Select from the various options or alternative solutions you've considered in Step 2 and decide which one best resolves the customer complaint. This is the one you propose. If you've read the situation correctly, considered the relevant facts, and weighed realistically each of the options or solutions that can work, the proposal you make will accomplish two important objectives:

1. It will satisfy the complaint, thereby reestablishing the customer's sense of "value received" that prompted him to buy from you originally. Indeed, a complaint-solving proposal may be so creative that it actually enhances that sense of value received.
2. It will reestablish your position as a supplier of value. It will reassert your capabilities and enhance your credibility. If the solution you propose is creative enough, it can even increase your business or improve your competitive standing.

Principles for Handling Complaints

In handling complaints you should observe the following general principles:

1. **If the complaint is made to you personally, hear it out.** Don't interrupt the speaker. Sometimes the very fact that one gets the complaint "off his chest" relieves some of the distress or ill feelings he has. And even if it doesn't, the more he talks, the more you will learn about what concerns him and how to deal with it. It may be uncomfortable, even unpleasant. But listen.

2. **Avoid getting into an argument.** The complaint may be groundless. It may be based on out-of-date information; don't make an issue of it. Complaints are not resolved to mutual satisfaction in a controversial climate.

3. **Don't make lame or meaningless excuses.** Excuses such as the following, are meaningless, and they do nothing to resolve the situation:

"We're no worse than anyone else on meeting schedules."
"But you've never complained before!"
"It's summertime you know, and that means we've got people skipping out early or taking a four-day weekend."

If the complaint is valid and the fault is yours, admit it, and admit it with no alibis. Face up to the problem you've caused, and assure the customer you'll get the facts and do your best to resolve the matter satisfactorily.

4. **Don't let complaints linger.** The longer they remain unresolved, the more complaints become a source of friction. The longer they are unsatisfied, the more apt they are to become serious. And once they get serious, they become a matter of official concern. A complaint from the maintenance foreman may be a minor problem to resolve now. However, once it gets the attention of the manufacturing manager, the purchasing manager, or higher management, it takes on totally different proportions.

5. **Remember, you're still selling value.** Just as the value selling concept is important to the original sale, it is equally important to satisfying complaints. The customer or buying influence who raises the complaint perceived value in the original buying decision. He saw his requirements satisfied and he saw them satisfied at the lowest cost in use. Therefore, any solution you propose must reestablish that sense of value received. It must satisfy his needs and it must be cost-effective.

The following two scenarios illustrate the value selling approach to handling complaints. See if you can recognize the value selling elements in each:

Scenario 1

JANE TRAYMOR, PRODUCT MANAGER FOR KAYZEE PET FOODS: I've called you in, Mr. Harper, because, since your company's become a source, we've had nothing but problems with your bags. We're getting complaint after complaint from customers about our pet food spoiling because after the bag is open it won't reclose. And I want to know what you're going to do about it.

ANDREW HARPER, SALESPERSON: I know about your problem, Ms. Traymor. Jack Malloy, your packaging engineer, has been on the phone with me almost steadily over the past four days. And I think we're going to come up with a way of solving it. But first let me point out a couple of facts to you:

1. All of Kayzee's pet food containers are built to Kayzee design. The bags we supply are produced to your drawings and to your specifications.

2. Although we're packaging designers as well as bag manufacturers, at no time did anyone at Kayzee ask our opinion
on what the bags should look like. In fact, when we tried
to make some suggestions to Malloy's predecessor, Marty
Latham, we were told he wasn't interested.

Anyway, here's what we've come up with. Instead of using
the interlaced twine or cord you now use to seal the bag, we've
come up with a simple plastic zipper that reseals the bag once
it's open. This will keep Rover's food nice and dry and smelling
as fresh as the day it was bought. And this will mean fewer
complaints, fewer returns, fewer order cancellations. As a matter
of fact, Ms. Traymor, it should give you a very marketable
feature on all the products you sell.

Scenario 2

JAMES WYATT, PLANT MANAGER FOR PANATONE ELECTRONICS.
I received your notice of a rate increase, and I want you to
know I don't like it. Our shipping costs are going through
the roof, and with business the way it is I can't take another
rate hike.

BILL ADAIR, SALESPERSON. I appreciate your situation, Mr. Wyatt,
but we're not singling you out for the increase. This is an
increase to all of our customers and merely puts us in line
with the rates now being charged by other shippers. Also, I'd
like to point out, it's not an across-the-board increase that
applies to all our classifications and all our services. Some things
have gone up; others remain the same; and a few have actually
come down.

Unfortunately, Mr. Wyatt, there's nothing we can do about
the rates. But there's a lot we can do about your shipping and
delivery costs. You know, in reviewing our experience with
Panatone we see an exceptionally high number of shipments
going out via overnight air express. That's the most expensive
way to ship. Yet, it's no guarantee that your package will get
there any sooner. Now let me propose this. We will perform
a detailed analysis of your package-shipping practices. We'll
study not only your priority shipments but all shipments. And
we'll look at the inbound as well as outbound. We'll compare
actual shipping modes with alternative forms of delivery, taking
into consideration their degree of urgency, package weights,
zone breaks, and comparative costs. If our experience with other

customers is any yardstick, we'll find substantial opportunities for savings despite the fact that the rates themselves may be higher. Just to give you an example that's in your own backyard:

Two months ago, we made the same kind of analysis for the Grimsby Company in Roxbury, one-half mile down the road from you. As a result of our findings, we set up with them three levels of priority that now apply to all their deliveries or shipments. With a small adhesive label we color code each package to identify its priority level. Code Red has the highest priority. It applies to an urgent shipment, such as a test sample or a critical-shortage item at a customer location. It goes out overnight express.

Code Yellow hasn't got the urgency of Code Red but still demands reasonably prompt delivery. It would apply for a shipment where the customer's running out but has a couple days' supply still on hand. Code Yellow is still second-day air delivery but is 70 percent less than overnight air express.

Code Blue applies to any package that does not demand the Red or Yellow priority. Code Blue packages will still reach their destination in five days or less. But costs run 90 percent lower than they do on overnight air delivery.

I'm sorry we can't reduce our rates, Mr. Wyatt, but if you'll allow us to work with you, we can definitely reduce your costs.

Handling Customer Changes

Customer changes are a common occurrence in industrial and institutional markets. They occur because the customer buys to satisfy requirements created by his product, process, or market and competitive demands. As those demands change, his purchase requirements change. The changes may be in designs or specifications. They may be in quantity, delivery, or completion dates. Regardless of the nature of the change in purchase requirements, that change alters the conditions of the original sale. It introduces factors that the seller was not required to consider originally.

Obviously, not all changes have the same effect on the seller's situation. Many changes are minor and will have no adverse impact on the seller's time, cost, or resource utilization. Changing the delivery from May 10 to May 9 may be of little or no consequence. Similarly, changing container markings from one description to another may be so minor as to be of no consequence. But changing an item's design when units made to the old design are completed or in production is another matter. Here production time is lost, and facilities have been employed and cost incurred on units that are now obsolete.

In handling changes you must assume that the initial sale satisfied the customer's requirements as they were originally defined. It satisfied the customer's perceptions of value—value in use, value in meeting the intended purpose of the purchase. In return, you agreed to a price—a value in exchange. When the customer seeks to change the conditions of the original transaction, legally and in equity there is a basis for changing the price or conditions of sale. Value given demands value in return. Changes in value given demand changes in value returned. That is fundamental to true value selling.

There are two approaches that salespeople often take toward customer changes, and neither is consistent with value selling. The first is to see the change as an opportunity to exploit the customer, to take advantage of his predicament and extract from him all that the situation will allow. The second is to rationalize the change by incorporating it as part of the original sale and justifying the action as "customer service." Let's consider each of these in more detail.

To begin with, the first approach is less the doing of salespeople than it is of Marketing or General Management. Using customer changes as an opportunity to exploit the customer reflects a calculated marketing and pricing strategy. And this is an activity outside the scope of the typical salesperson's responsibility. Nevertheless, salespeople can influence that strategy. Certainly, they have to live with its consequences, so any practice that endangers the customer-seller relationship must become a matter of sales concern.

It has been my experience that the practice of using changes to exploit the customer is more common in industries like military and government contracting, building and construction, and capital equipment production and related services than elsewhere. And there are two common elements in all these industries that make that so:

1. These industries rely heavily, and in some instances totally, on competitive bidding as the principal method of source selection and price determination. Accordingly, there is a strong temptation for sellers to bid low—that is to "buy in"—and then recoup what they did not allow in the original price by overpricing changes. Many of the so-called cost overruns on military projects are prime cases in point. If those projects had been realistically estimated and priced initially, they never would have been funded. Therefore, the strategy is to buy in, then make up the difference on the engineering changes.

2. Procurement in these industries is casual or intermittent. There is little or no planned long-term relationship between buyer and seller. In fact, in government business this is prohibited because each procurement must be competitively bid or negotiated as a separate and distinct commitment.

Where the buyer-seller relationship is a casual or one-time one, there is that same temptation to exploit the customer, because he may not be around tomorrow. The reasoning is "get all you can when you can." The serious consequence of this strategy to the salesperson is that it tends to promote an adversarial climate for selling. The strategy can be highly effective in recouping those unallowed-for dollars in the original price. And it may even go unchallenged for a time. But ultimately, the customer will react and react in kind. If he concludes he's been exploited, he'll play the same game. He will demand that the seller justify the price he asks for the change by breaking it down into specific elements and details of cost, overhead, and profit. He will issue change notices to the supplier on a "no charge" basis, throwing the burden back on the seller to disprove the justification of the "no charge." He will withhold payments if the supplier does not agree to his estimates of what a reasonable price for the change should be. He will claim that the change was unauthorized; that it was not in writing or did not follow formal purchasing procedures; and therefore, legally, that it was not a valid and supportable claim.

The second common approach to handling changes is equally faulty. Indeed, it may be more damaging than the first. At least the first approach does not jeopardize seller costs and profit. Its aim is to improve both. But when we view the implementing of changes as a "service" to be given away for nothing, we jeopardize both costs and profit. We also lose the opportunity to reinforce our position as a value contributor, because things given away are never fully appreciated.

Treating a change as a service to be given away is a common problem because salespeople are in a better position to employ this approach. Whereas few salespeople can initiate and effect the first approach—that is, exploiting the customer—many can succumb to the second. They are in constant contact with the customer's people. They provide technical information, samples, and test results; they monitor production or expedite delivery; they take units off machines or production lines and hand carry them to the customer to satisfy some urgent need. In so doing they can easily identify with customer personnel or with customer interests. In time they can even see themselves in the role of a customer advocate.

Now this is not to say that salespeople ought not provide the kind of services suggested above. On the contrary, and most emphatically, servicing the account well is as important a selling responsibility as making the sale initially. But the line between providing the service value we originally sold and giving the store away can easily get blurred. When that happens we make customer changes without considering their cost or adverse consequence to us. When that happens we enhance value that the customer receives with no acknowledgment or reciprocal benefit in return. And that is not value selling.

We said earlier that customer changes can be opportunities in disguise. They become opportunities because when we handle and implement them effectively, we enhance value contribution to the customer. Like objections and complaints, changes are a reflection of customer-perceived problems. Unlike objections and complaints, however, changes are problems that the customer perceives as his own doing. He makes a change in design or specification. But he knows it was his design or specification that created the problem to begin with. He makes a change in quantity or delivery rates. But it was his original schedule that created the availability problem. For this reason, the customer's attitude toward the seller is totally different on the matter of changes than it is on objections and complaints. He is not hostile. He is not adversarial. He wants cooperation. He even welcomes recommendations and advice.

Now obviously, not all changes have the same degree of urgency. There are design or specification changes that are critical to the customer's product integrity or process performance. These are incorporated immediately. Similarly, there are changes that affect purchase quantities or delivery rates. And these also can become critical, as when a customer's market evaporates, or his inventory demands disappear or suddenly explode. These changes, too, are made immediately.

But for the largest number of changes the customer may consider, there is an exercise he goes through before he actually effects the change. First, he evaluates the change in terms of its technical merits and the timing for its implementation. Second, he assesses the impact of the change on all factors that are affected. Will it make inventory obsolete or existing quantities excessive? What will it do to schedules? What will it cost? And clearly, if the change applies to a purchased item, he must go through that same exercise and ask those same questions of the supplier. When he does, you have the opportunity to enhance value contribution to the customer and value in exchange to yourself.

EXAMPLE: Markel Motors bought valves in various sizes and quantities from H & G Manufacturing. Because of cost considerations, Markel had always specified packaging and shipping instructions to its suppliers. In the case of the valves, they not only specified the material and construction of the shipping crate but they also directed that the valves be shipped in Markel's trucks. Markel maintained a small fleet of cars and trucks it used to pick up parts and components from its suppliers, as well as to make small deliveries within the area. Accordingly, H & G's valves were sharing space not only with paper and paperboard cartons but also with castings, extrusions, and heavy machined parts.

When the valves reached Markel's plant they were often scratched or their protective wrapping was damaged, so a specification change was called for in the material or construction of the shipping crate. Markel's intention was to use heavier board for the crating and to reinforce valve separators so that the valves would not bang against each other in transit.

The salesperson who handled the Markel account was Charlie Sylverson. Charlie had handled the account for five years and was thoroughly familiar with how Markel received the valves, how they stored them, and how they used them. He had thought about the problem for a long time, so when he was asked about the intended change, he was more than ready to express his thoughts. On a yellow writing pad, Charlie sketched out a combination shipping and receiving container that would be inserted within the currently used wooden crate. The container would be a wire-bound box with a base that would act as a skid once it was removed from the crate. Valves would be strapped or taped to the skid so that each container and skid could hold six different sizes of valves firmly in place. Charlie explained that the same base of this wire-bound box that served as a shipper could be used to move valves around from receiving through inspection and through the assembly process where the valves and motors were assembled. Charlie estimated that savings from this proposed change would be:

- A reduction of fifteen minutes per crate to remove the valves in the wire-bound box compared with the existing crate design
- A savings of one hour per valve in moving valves from receiving through assembly
- A reduction in damages and returns of at least 50 percent

Within three months from the time that Charlie's suggestions were implemented, Markel reported savings better than Charlie had estimated and damages in transit were reduced to zero.

As a result of Charlie's effective handling of the change, Markel received enhanced value. H&G Manufacturing got value in exchange with a 5 percent price increase to cover the cost of the wire-bound box and skid base, and a 50 percent increase in Markel's valve business. Value to the customer was enhanced. Value in exchange to the seller was also enhanced.

Here are three points to keep in mind whenever you deal with customer-initiated changes:

1. Handling changes is an unavoidable and necessary part of the industrial selling job. It's just another phase of the selling process, another step in maintaining and cultivating the customer account. As

such, you must apply the same value selling principles to handling changes as you did to the initial sale. Your aim is still to satisfy customer requirements, to relate your product features and company capabilities to those requirements, and to mesh the two with cost-effectiveness.

2. Since customer changes alter the original conditions surrounding the sale, you must assess them not only in terms of the customer's requirements but also in terms of how they affect you. Do they conflict with your best interest? Is the customer asking you to do something you shouldn't do? For example, if the customer asks you to make a design or material change that in your experienced opinion will not work, it's not in your best interests to proceed blindly. Under those circumstances you should resist the change. If the change is one to the customer's design, you may ultimately be forced to implement it. But as a value seller you must challenge the change. And you should do so by providing meaningful explanations as to why. The only meaningful explanations are that the customer's requirements will not be satisfied or that the change will not be cost-effective. In other words, it will not contribute value.

3. As a value seller you must look at changes as an opportunity to enhance not only value contribution to the customer but also value in exchange to yourself. Again, value given demands value in return; it may take the form of higher prices, additional business, or merely acknowledgment in considering future business, but there must be some reciprocal benefit or advantage. Value sellers never give anything away, because they know that what is given away has no worth in the eyes of the recipient.

Chapter 8

ESTABLISHING CREDIBILITY IN VALUE SELLING

Since value is the satisfaction of customer requirements at the lowest total cost in use, it is realized (or not realized) only after the supplier performs. Although it is perceived by the customer at the time of sale, it is only experienced in the use or application of what the customer receives. If what he receives meets quality and time requirements and proves cost-effective, value has been supplied. If what he receives does not meet requirements or is not cost-effective, value has not been supplied. The confirmation of value, therefore, is in seller performance. And the credibility of the seller as a value supplier is a direct function of that performance.

But credibility as a value supplier is also a function of the salesperson's performance. It is the salesperson who sells the promise of value to begin with. It is the salesperson who represents and commits the seller to supplying it. Hence, it is understandable that it is the salesperson the customer looks to when value is not supplied or is in jeopardy.

This is particularly true in industrial markets where requirements are often unique. Here, the salesperson does not merely "write up an order." He interprets those unique requirements; he may even help define them. He also translates them back to those who design, produce, or perform to satisfy them. In brief, he is an important and highly visible link in the process of supplying value. When that process fails, it is not surprising that the customer sees the salesperson as also failing.

To illustrate, here's what the head of Materials and Procurement for a large corporation in the aerospace and electronics industry said about the salesperson's role:

> Industrial salesmen—the men we see in our offices every day— have one major fault, I believe. It's not backdoor selling, ignorance of the product, neglecting to get an appointment, or any of the other shortcomings of which we are aware.
>
> It's simply this: a strikingly obvious failure to analyze the unique requirements of every individual customer.
>
> Most salesmen fall down on the areas of quality and delivery requirements. On top of this they don't . . . pass on this pertinent data to their own manufacturing and inspection departments. The net result—operating departments in the vendor's plant never get accurate information about customer's needs, which results in unnecessary cancellations, rejections, and bad feelings.

Now it may be clear to the individual quoted that the failure to supply value is first and foremost attributable to the salesperson, and it may well be that his personal experience justifies the comment. But as a general assessment, the criticism is harsh and probably exaggerated. Nevertheless, it demands attention because (1) it is not an isolated opinion, and (2) it reflects a view of the sales responsibility that salespeople may not recognize or acknowledge.

Although the quotation cited was made by an executive with responsibilities for Materials and Procurement, criticism of salespeople is not confined to that functional area alone. Indeed, complaints about inattention to specification details are more common and vehement from customer engineering or technical people than they are from Purchasing. And complaints about poor coordination between the customer and the supplier's manufacturing or quality control personnel are more frequently heard from customer production or marketing people. So the statement ought not be dismissed as just another "Purchasing gripe."

Recently, I witnessed an example of what becomes a clear cause for customer dissatisfaction with the salesperson's performance. A client in the computer industry contracted to buy a quantity of parts that were to be gold-plated. The specifications called for a 0.0002 inch minimum thickness of gold plate throughout the part. This requirement was not only pointed out but also stressed to the supplier's salesman. When the parts came in they were carefully inspected and rejected. It was found that they had not been produced with a 0.0002 minimum gold thickness. They were produced with an *average* thickness of 0.0002. Whether it was a case of the salesperson's not writing the order correctly, or his plant producing what was less costly or more convenient to make, I cannot say. But I can say that the customer was definitely dissatisfied with the salesman. And that dissatisfaction was expressed not only in Purchasing. In fact, long before Purchasing even learned of the problem, the salesman was in the doghouse with both Quality Control and Production. I can also say that as a result of that incident both the salesman and his company lost credibility—he as the person who made the sale, and his company as the seller who contracted for value but failed to supply it.

Credibility of the Salesperson in Selling Value

Credibility is simply believability. It is the faculty to command confidence or inspire trust and thus has a personal and emotional dimension. The very presence or physical appearance of some people can be a source of comfort and reassurance, while the manner or bearing of others can be a source of uneasiness or doubt. Words and the phrasing of words can evoke a sympathetic or a guarded response. The inflection we give to a word, our look, our facial expression can all trigger reactions of suspicion or belief. For these reasons, salespeople should pay close attention to their personal appearance, dress, speech pattern, and general demeanor. These strengthen or weaken a person's image of credibility.

But the substance of that credibility is the salesperson's performance. And this gets back to the view we hold of the sales responsibility. How do we as salespeople see the selling function, and is it consistent with the customer's view? What do we see as activities we must perform? What are activities we should perform in order to fulfill our role as the customer perceives it? If what we see as our function and what we do in performing it do not conform to what the customer expects, we have an obvious condition for damaging—or never establishing—credibility.

So where and how do salespeople fall short in fulfilling the responsibilities that the customer expects from them? And what are specific areas of selling failure?

On the basis of what I've learned as a purchasing consultant to major corporations, I would include the following:

Lack of product or service knowledge. Product or service knowledge is so essential to industrial selling that one may question the seriousness of this charge. But lack of depth in knowing and understanding the product or service that salespeople sell is one of the most common criticisms made by customer buying influences. Obviously, this is not a criticism of all salespeople, or of salespeople in any particular industry. But there seems to be a pattern. The problem tends to be more acute in industries that use advanced technology. It is more apt to be a problem in computer and computer services, specialized engineering and professional services, and electronics, biotechnology, and telecommunications than it is in mature or commodity industries like steel and paper. Perhaps it is the rate of technological change that makes it difficult to learn and assimilate what is needed to become knowledgeable, let alone expert, in what one sells. In any event, knowledge—or the lack of it—is a critical factor in the customer's appraisal of performance.

Knowledge of the customer's applications. An equally common criticism of salespeople is their lack of detailed information and understanding of the customer's requirements. The stories are countless of salespeople walking into buying offices and asking, "What do you do or make here?" The fact that this should have been known before the salesperson called is obvious enough to shrug the matter off as just "dumb selling." But what cannot be shrugged off is the harm done by those who sell with little understanding of the customer's application. That harm is not only to the company they represent, but also to the customer. And this can happen with salespeople who know what they're selling as well as those who don't. Indeed, one of the serious failings of much sales training is the stress it places on product knowledge alone. I may know as much as can be known about the product I sell, what it does and how it does it. But if I don't understand the special and unique requirements of my customer's application, I am an ineffectual salesman. The fact that I sell 10-HPW motors and I know in detail what they do and how they do it is not the only important consideration. What is also important is that I know what the customer's power requirements call for. Does the customer's application really involve a 10-HPW load?

Lack of knowledge or understanding of the customer's business. Knowing the customer's business is knowing more than the technical demands of his application. It means knowing his production and inventory needs—his forecasts, his production schedules, his quality and delivery requirements. It means knowing the customer's markets, how they behave, and how they affect and are affected by what we supply. It means knowing the special or unique demands those markets impose on a customer for product quality, product improvement, reliability of supply, product training, and financing. The more the salesperson knows and understands about the customer's business, the more credible he becomes as a seller of value.

One of the most powerful sales presentations I ever heard was by the regional sales manager for a manufacturer of chemical processing equipment. This salesperson had so thoroughly researched the customer's business that he sold with authority. He knew the customer's sales forecasts and the production quantities and rates needed to support those forecasts. He knew projected price levels on the product to be sold. He knew rates of return on assets and sales that the customer employed in decisions of this type. He knew money rates and the payback formulas the customer would use in justifying the purchase. And he tailored his presentation to use every piece of customer knowledge he had with maximum effect. He closed the sale because he was knowledgeable. And because he was knowledgeable he was credible.

Lack of attention to details. The example where parts were gold-plated with an average rather than a minimum thickness of 0.0002 inch is a good case in point. Whether it was an error in writing the specifications or a failure to follow up production, the customer attributed the rejection to the salesperson's lack of attention to detail. In this case it was a failure in interpretation, translation, or follow-up of specifications. But lack of attention to detail is manifest in other ways as well—mathematical errors in quotations, missing zeroes or misplaced decimal points, insufficient documentation to support quotations, omissions of pertinent data, or faulty contract language. Lack of concern with detail is always time-consuming, because what is missing or faulty must be supplied or corrected later. And it is also costly. Further, when the salesperson causes the customer additional time and cost, his credibility as a value seller suffers.

Failure to provide meaningful and timely information. Nothing is more irritating than the salesperson who calls on the customer with nothing meaningful to say. Idle chatter about baseball scores and golf tournaments is a waste of customer time. And social chitchat to cover up real lack of product or service knowledge is an affront to the customer's technical and professional concerns. As one production manager put it: "No amount of personal effervescence or conversation will ever sell a product for industrial use."

The customer rightly looks to the salesperson as a source of information. He wants to learn about the latest technical developments and to hear about similar applications in related industries or situations. He wants to be kept abreast of market changes, future supply and demand conditions, impending price adjustments.

The customer looks to the salesperson for advice. When a distribution manager or the buyer for an industrial supply chain buys thousands of MRO items, he cannot be an expert on them all. He relies on the salesperson to recommend items to stock up on, items to promote, items to mark down or liquidate. The more helpful the salesperson is in providing meaningful information, the more the customer will look to him for recommendations and advice.

Failure to follow through after the sale is made. Although suppliers may distinguish between Sales and Customer Service, the customer does not necessarily recognize that distinction. He still looks to the salesperson as the one responsible for servicing his account. And servicing that account means taking personal responsibility to assure that values sold are in fact supplied. Specifically, this means following up on the performance of those who produce or supply what was sold;

reporting progress—or lack of it—as soon as it is known; and providing realistic information as to what the customer can expect, and when. It means clearly and openly reporting problems that threaten successful completion, rather than hiding them or covering them up. Again, industrial customers are not surprised by problems. They expect them to occur and they establish plans and options to implement if and when they do occur. But what makes the customer furious is being smooth-talked into believing that everything is fine, and then learning too late that it's not.

Now for the most part, customer buying influences recognize the limits and constraints on the salesperson's ability to ensure performance. They fully appreciate that once the purchase order is signed, the actual implementation of its terms is the responsibility of the supplier's technical, professional, or operating people. But customers do expect that the salesperson be willing to extend himself personally in following up on the sale. And success in doing so is an important measure of his credibility as a value seller.

Failure to follow up with the customer's specifiers or users on what was sold. A common and justified criticism about salespeople is that once they've made the sale, their interest and concern with the customer ceases. As many of us can testify, this is an all-too-common occurrence in consumer markets, where, once we buy the stereo, the automobile, or the household appliance, the salesperson who sold them seems to forget we ever existed. He makes no effort to learn how the product works, or if it works at all. Are we happy with its features? Does it do all he said it would do? As distressing as that sales behavior may be, we all have come to live with it and chalk it off to the times, to society, to changing work and social ethics.

But in industrial markets, that behavior is not easily accepted or condoned. Industrial customers expect salespeople to follow up on the sale they've made. They expect them to inquire as to whether the specifications defined have in fact been met and whether performance conforms to design or application requirements. They also expect that salespeople make it their business to know how the product is used, how it is handled and stored, and how it is employed with other items of purchase or customer manufacture. Customers expect to be told when they don't operate or maintain what they've bought the way the supplier recommends. They expect to be shown the correct way. And they expect that salespeople will be constantly alert to identify new applications or uses for what they sell, based on the knowledge and experience they've gained with what they have already sold.

Failure to honor commitments or keep their word. Although failure to honor commitments is a shortcoming of relatively few salespeople, it ranks high as a source of customer dissatisfaction. It does so because, on the basis of the salesperson's word, customer buying influences make judgments and decisions. They commit themselves to others—internally to other functions; externally to their customers, other suppliers, and government or regulatory agencies.

- When the salesperson fails to get quotations in when and in the manner promised, he may limit the customer's ability to quote to his customer in a timely or realistic fashion.
- When the salesperson assures the customer that he will submit or return drawings or specifications by a given date and fails to do so, he can jeopardize engineering or manufacturing schedules. He can even create customer inspection and quality control problems.
- When the salesperson promises to supply product, performance, or cost information that must be reported to government agencies or investigative or regulatory bodies and is late in doing so, the customer is exposed to possible damages or penalties.

The very essence of credibility is that one can be trusted. The salesperson who promises what he cannot deliver, or commits himself to an objective he cannot achieve, is not trustworthy; nor is the salesperson who learns and discloses to others technical or other information that the customer considers confidential or solely for his own internal use. In today's technologically explosive markets, this practice is a growing cause for concern. And to the customer, it is an important test of every salesperson's credibility.

Failure to recognize or comply with customer policies, procedures, or protocol. Every company establishes policies and procedures concerning its purchasing and its commitments to outside suppliers. Policies cover matters such as levels of buying authority, evaluation and selection of sources, and recommended and restricted buying practices. Procedures define methods of requisitioning, bid solicitation, bid evaluation, purchase order placement, acknowledgment, and so on. Protocol is the etiquette or code of behavior customer personnel recognize among themselves in matters dealing with outside suppliers. For example, it may be protocol that the purchasing department be informed when the product or design engineer contacts an outside supplier for cost or delivery information or for samples. It may be protocol that when a meeting is held between the customer's and the supplier's technical people, the purchasing agent who buys the item discussed be invited to attend.

A source of customer criticism is the salesperson's ignoring or evading those buying policies, procedures, or protocol. Admittedly, it is the customer's purchasing department that is most vocal in leveling that criticism. And, in some cases, it can be exaggerated, even petty and parochial. But probably every major company has been burned at one time or another by their people making commitments to suppliers without authorization. And it is for this reason that purchasing policies and procedures are established. Obviously they are binding only on the customer's people. But it is an element of the salesperson's credibility that he learn and understand what they are, and that he be trustworthy in complying with them.

Failure to recognize changing customer priorities; failure to report them back to supplier management. Customer perceptions of what is important change as technical or business considerations change. And the criticism made of salespeople is that:

- They are unaware of such changes and their implications; or
- They do not communicate back those changes and what they imply to both the customer and the company they represent

To illustrate:

EXAMPLE 1: The customer inaugurates a quality improvement program. Her objective is to reduce rejections by a quantum rate. In so doing, she tells you of her plans to establish process and inspection controls over the critical items she buys When customer engineering and quality people arrive at your plant, it is to the complete surprise of your production and management people. You never understood the demands of improved supplier quality, or you failed to communicate them back to your own management.

EXAMPLE 2: The customer reorganizes his purchasing function. Where before he bought through a centralized commodity specialist, he now buys through decentralized project or division buyers. An important implication of this change is that the requirements and priorities of those decentralized buyers are different from those of the centralized commodity specialist. The salesperson who is unaware of the change or fails to notify his company of it jeopardizes the caliber and amount of servicing the customer account will receive.

EXAMPLE 3: The customer's immediate concern is cost reduction. In pursuing it, he invites suggestions from suppliers for cost-saving steps they can take. He asks for their cooperation in improving product design, methods of manufacture, and methods of packing and shipping, all with the aim of reducing costs. The salesperson either dismisses what he hears as "the same old story, not worth getting anybody's feathers ruffled about," or he deliberately withholds the information for fear of what it may mean to his job status or job security.

Salespeople who are credible as value sellers are true professionals. They are knowledgeable about both what they sell and what the customer requires. They are alert to changes that affect both. They are attuned to the customer—his people, his practices, his problems—and are skilled in interpreting what they hear or learn. They communicate back to responsible plant, office, or management people the information that they have gathered, the unpleasant as well as the pleasant. They are catalysts who bring together the resources of the company they represent with the appropriate buying influences who specify, use, or otherwise affect purchasing decisions. And they see the selling function as value contributing and value enhancing.

Skills of the Professional Salesperson

There are certain skills that all salespeople must possess, and these are presented in ample detail in any number of books, audiocassettes, videotapes, and training programs. They are the skills of effective communication, of understanding and applying the principles and techniques of motivation. They are more particular selling skills, such as prospecting for new customers, getting their attention, or closing the sale. And because they are so well and fully treated elsewhere, there is no purpose in treating them again here. Some skills, however, are special to value selling, and because they are, they deserve special consideration. They are skills the true professional constantly sharpens and applies, and they include skill in assessing correctly the customer and the sales situation; skill in harmonizing requirements of the customer with the interests and concerns of his own people; and skill in closing the loop from sale to customer satisfaction.

Correct Assessment of the Customer and the Sales Situation

The salesperson becomes an effective value contributor when he sizes up the customer and sales situation correctly. He does so by:

1. *Knowing who customer buying influences are—what their interests and concerns may be; how they are likely to be reflected in the current sale.* The skilled salesperson correctly evaluates the relative importance and authority of buying influences. He is constantly aware of any changes in their position, status, or area of responsibility.

2. *Assessing every sales situation in terms of customer policies, practices, or preferences.* Does the customer buy on a hand-to-mouth basis? Does he do any planned or forward buying? Is he receptive to alternative proposals and specifications, terms, and conditions different from those on a standard purchase order form? The skilled salesperson assesses each sales situation in terms of how the customer acts or reacts to general market conditions and how he conforms or deviates from past buying patterns.

3. *Anticipating customer requirements.* The skilled salesperson is objective in evaluating specifications, bills of materials, and descriptions and definitions of work scope. He is knowledgeable in determining when they are necessary, marginally useful, functionally useless, or redundant. He is authoritative in expressing his opinions and point of view.

4. *Distinguishing carefully between customer conduct and concern on a specific transaction and customer behavior and priorities over the long term.* Under compelling circumstances, every customer will pursue objectives that are at variance with those he normally pursues. Even the most ardent advocate of quality assurance will at some point or other be forced to pursue supplier price concessions. It takes an astute eye to recognize when this is occurring and an experienced

judgment to know how to deal with it. The skilled salesperson has both.

5. *Knowing how to evaluate customer inquiries or requests for information.* Does the customer have a defined requirement, with money budgeted or appropriated for purchase, or is he merely seeking data for planning or estimating purposes? Is he looking for competitive information to use against other suppliers? Is he checking or validating information you gave him six months ago, a year ago? It makes a world of difference which motives influence the customer's inquiry or request. And the skilled salesperson will know how to respond to each.

6. *Placing proper worth on his company's product or service features, the caliber of its customer service, and its reputation for loyalty, integrity, and dependability.* The skilled salesperson doesn't exaggerate his company's strengths, but he doesn't ignore them either. He knows they are important in the customer's appraisal of competitive suppliers, and he presents his company's case with enthusiasm and confidence.

7. *Always checking with his own engineering, production, or operating people to make sure that their assessment of the sale is consistent or compatible with his own.* Does the new business fit in with the existing product or business mix? Are the demands for up-front engineering, tooling, or start-up acceptable? Or are they prohibitive? Are there planning or implementation problems he has not recognized, so that perhaps the sale should be reconsidered or even avoided? The skilled salesperson does not pursue business that is undesirable, or undeliverable.

8. *Correctly reading the signs showing how he stands competitively.* Is his company a preferred source? If so, why? Is his company a nonpreferred source? If so, why? What are the factors that will be critical in deciding who gets the customer's business, and how does his company rate on each? The salesperson who is skilled in making these assessments is worth his weight in gold.

9. *Knowing when and how to apply sales effort with customer buying influences other than his own immediate contact.* This is a delicate matter, and it calls for tact and finesse to carry off without adverse repercussions or personal resentment. The skilled salesperson is sensitive to the personal relationships in the sales situation.

10. *Knowing when and how to bring in his own technical specialists and operating or higher management to assist in the sales presentation or to help close the sale.* The skilled salesperson must weigh not only the contributions he can make to the sale but also the reactions of the customer to the presence and involvement of others. A miscalculation on either score can damage or kill the sale.

Skill in Harmonizing Customer Requirements With the Interests and Concerns of His Own People

The salesperson is an effective value contributor when he harmonizes the objectives of the customer with those of his company. He does so by:

1. **Maintaining close contact with those who specify and use.** The skilled salesperson is alert to all opportunities for influencing specifications or work scope descriptions to reflect his company's product and service strengths. He sees his role as that of consultant or advisor to the customer, guiding him to avoid problems and pitfalls in the task of defining product or service requirements.

2. **Placing strong importance on his company's technical, production, and management capabilities.** The skilled salesperson knows these are value contributing factors that the customer may not acknowledge. Nonetheless, they are essential to the satisfaction of both defined and implied requirements. A good salesperson is diligent in relating product features to the defined requirements. But he also knows that customer value is supplied or enhanced by supplier resources and capabilities that are not necessarily specified.

3. **Constantly seeking opportunities to sell-up.** The skilled salesperson is constantly aware of how he can enhance value to the customer, how he can enhance value in exchange to his company. Instead of selling single items, he sells packages or families of items. Instead of selling products, he sells systems. The thrust of his effort in selling-up, however, is always to enhance value, so he carefully avoids price as a customer consideration for buying-up. The skilled salesperson knows that a price concession for buying-up can be used to squeeze out further price concessions; and that selling up can be a double-edged sword. It can work for him, but it can also work against him.

4. **Making certain that when he sells-up, he has the under-standing, support, and cooperation of his own people.** Combining product items into packages or families demands coordinated planning and scheduling. Delivering systems demands systems engineering, systems production, and systems management and controls. These differ from the activities used to produce and deliver single products. Do his people want this kind of business? Can they handle it effectively? It is self-defeating for the salesperson to sell-up when his own people are unaware of the consequences or are not in full agreement with the objective.

5. **Making it his business to know who processes sales orders, who plans or schedules production, and who monitors and follows up on performance.** The skilled salesperson is careful not to become a nuisance in making inquiries or seeking information. But he knows he has a responsibility to keep his customer informed. He recognizes that communication is a two-way street, so if he seeks information from his plant or distribution people, he must also provide meaningful information back. Feedback of problems, customer complaints, and competitive intelligence are both wanted and needed. And the skilled salesperson knows that how he responds to those wants and needs will be a measure of his credibility to his own people.

6. **Making periodic trips back to the factory, the office, or the laboratory whenever the opportunity arises or whenever he can create the opportunity.** The effective salesperson knows that this is one of the best ways of learning firsthand the progress and problems on important customer orders. Where circumstances warrant, he arranges such visits with customer Personnel. He knows that face-to-face discussions between his own and the customer's technical or production people go a long way toward resolving problems quickly and effectively. But as a skilled salesperson, he also knows that for such visits to be successful, he must plan and supervise them to the last detail.

7. **Always being positive in his dealings with the customer and his own people.** Although the knowledge or information he transmits may be negative, the skilled salesperson puts it in a positive light.

EXAMPLE: "We've had a breakdown on the rotary blender we use to process your product materials, and this means we'll have to do some juggling and rescheduling. But we are taking the following steps and we believe they will avoid any serious delays. . . ."

Or there may be no information to report at all.

> EXAMPLE: "I've heard nothing from the customer on those change orders, but I'm right on top of the situation, and I promise you, you'll know as soon as I do.

Contributing value is a positive process, and the skilled value seller establishes a positive climate in order for that process to succeed.

Closing the Loop From Sale to Customer Satisfaction

The skilled salesperson knows that a value sale does not end with the order. You close the loop from sale to customer satisfaction by:

1. **Planning not only the sales presentation, but the necessary steps for ensuring performance after the sale is made.** A skilled salesperson knows that value is not realized until customer requirements are satisfied with cost-effectiveness. Hence, you must set priorities on after-sale goals and objectives, set time schedules for their attainment, and monitor results against plans.

2. **Carefully reading the customer's requirements—his design and material specifications, his descriptions and definitions of work scope.** In considering these requirements, the skilled salesperson assumes nothing. He checks for facts and makes certain that his understanding of the customer's demands is consistent with what the customer intends. He also carefully identifies customer buying motives and assesses them correctly. If, for example, price is a primary consideration, he relates that motive to all elements of the customer's demand. Quality assurance specified by a price buyer does not have the same meaning as quality assurance specified by a value buyer.

3. **Not forcing a buying decision if the timing is not right.** For value to be sold, the customer must be confident that what he agrees to buy will in fact be supplied. If he has any doubts that this will occur, he will be wary and expectant of failure. He will seize on

every problem as a confirmation of failure. The skilled salesperson knows when and how to press for a customer commitment, when and how to forestall it.

4. **Discouraging changes and alternative approaches after the sale is made.** Changes alter the original selling scenario. The skilled salesperson knows that they open up the sale to new assessments, new considerations. Unless changes can result in value enhancement to the customer and value enhancement in exchange to the supplier, he resists and opposes them.

5. **Keeping the customer informed of progress.** In some situations no news may be good news. But on critical or complex purchases, it can be a source of customer worry, suspicion, or doubt. The skilled salesperson knows that the customer needs reassurance, that he needs to know if and how his requirements are being met. By keeping him apprised of developments, the salesperson addresses both these needs.

6. **Making sure the customer knows the particulars of value that has been supplied—the what, the when, and the how of that value supplied.** The skilled salesperson makes sure the customer knows of his company's performance in meeting or surpassing the customer's quality and time requirements. He gains recognition of technical, professional, or management services provided over and above the product values specified. He identifies and quantifies contributions to customer cost savings, cost avoidance, and cost offsets. In brief, he confirms and gains acknowledgment that value sold was in fact supplied.

7. **Continually improving his knowledge of the product and the customer as well as his value selling skills.** The skilled salesperson knows that every sales situation is a learning or reinforcing experience. He extracts new principles from new situations. He strengthens old principles he has learned before. He applies both old and new in a never-ending learning process whose objectives are:

- Value to the customer
- Value in exchange to his company

Credibility of the Company as A Supplier of Value

As the saying goes, "The proof of the pudding is in the eating." So it is with company credibility. The proof that the company is a value supplier is in its performance. To the customer, the demands of that performance are straightforward. They entail consistent satisfaction of requirements for quality, quantity, and time. They entail satisfaction of those requirements at the lowest cost in use. Customers express buying preferences on the basis of perceived differences in usefulness or cost-effectiveness. The past performance of suppliers in meeting those objectives, therefore, is the acid test of their credibility.

But how does the customer—or more correctly, how do customer buying influences—know what a supplier's past performance has been? How can the customer differentiate among several suppliers, all supplying the same item concurrently? Are its definitions of "performance" clear enough to know what it's measuring? Can the customer capture data that realistically reflect the "performance" he wishes to measure? Does he have reliable systems that enable him to update, analyze, and report "performance results"? Do the customer's suppliers know and understand how they are being measured, and is their performance in fact affected by how the customer rates them?

There are different approaches to supplier evaluation, and it is important that salespeople know what they are and how they are applied. The approaches range from ones that are highly subjective to computerized systems that record and report factual data. Let's look at how they work.

Consensus Evaluation

The simplest and probably the most frequently used method of supplier performance evaluation is consensus evaluation. It relies heavily on the opinions and experience of customer's personnel who influence or make buying decisions. Functionally, they are managers responsible for purchasing, quality control, production or inventory control, or other activities that can assess vendor performance.

Every month or quarter, the purchasing department (or whatever function is charged with the task) calls a meeting to evaluate supplier performance over the past period. The meeting includes all those who collected performance data or are affected by supplier performance. From that data, as well as from personal experience and opinion, each participant rates suppliers by company standards. Ratings may be a numerical ranking (one, two, and three) or they may be expressed as "favorable-unfavorable" or perhaps as "positive-negative-neutral." If the consensus from these ratings is unfavorable or negative, the supplier is notified and asked to explain. In most cases, he is given an opportunity to improve his performance. But if he fails to do so in subsequent periods, he receives a smaller share of business or may be dropped as an active source.

In larger companies, the consensus approach to vendor rating is used only on one-time or intermittent purchases. For large-quantity, repetitive purchases, the evaluation of suppliers is too complex and potentially too controversial to allow for subjective opinion. The consensus approach is seen as too informal, too unstructured for the controlled financial and accounting demands of the large-company environment. Further, performance classifications are too general and rating criteria too broad to be authoritative and hence acceptable to all buying influences. As a consequence, the large company uses other approaches to supplier performance rating and these we will consider later in this chapter.

In smaller companies the consensus approach is popular because it is simple to use, yet considered adequate for its purpose. In small companies there is close and frequent contact among all those who specify, use, and buy. There is more common knowledge and understanding of what suppliers do or don't do. Thus, there is less concern that the experience or opinions of individual raters might be uninformed, misinformed, or biased. The very fact that these individuals are in close and constant contact with each other makes the consensus approach acceptable to them all.

For this reason the person who sells to smaller companies should keep in close touch with all those who contribute to the vendor rating consensus. He can learn of problems before they become general knowledge and resolve them before they become serious. He can address questions of quality or time performance and answer, clarify, or correct them personally and quickly. Because consensus evaluation is subjective, he can influence judgments and opinions. The attitude and actions of the salesperson are a more important factor of supplier credibility to the small customer than to the large.

Now obviously, the salesperson must do no less in the large company than in the small. He must make the same efforts at keeping in touch and working closely with buying influences and must cultivate and develop personal relations. But he must also recognize that the large company does not evaluate suppliers by opinion alone; its approach is more formalized and systematized. It relies less on subjective impressions or feelings than on factual and statistical evidence. The large company does not identify credibility as a value supplier with the salesperson's performance, but rather with the supplier's, although in fact the two may be intimately intertwined. And he rates that performance in objective and impersonal terms. Following are two such approaches to that rating.

Weighted-Point System

Quality, price, and delivery are cited as the prime considerations of value to the customer. Accordingly, in evaluating suppliers, the weighted-point system ascribes a weighing factor to each of these three areas of supplier performance. The system allows personal opinion and judgment in the definition of performance factors and the selection of performance indicators, as well as in the assignment of weights to each factor. These opinions and judgments are reduced to consensus ones, and they are reflected in the system's design details. But once the system and its details are established, personal opinion and judgment no longer influence the ratings or scores achieved.

The simplest definition of quality is conformance to specification. Hence, the weighted-point system measures quality performance by determining the number of units or lot shipments accepted and rejected out of the total number received. If 100 units are received and 10 are rejected, the unweighted quality rating is 90.

Price is unit price less discounts plus transportation charges for a net price. And it is rated supplier by supplier. Thus, the lowest net price has an unweighted rating of 100 and all higher prices are factored downward accordingly.

The system defines delivery as compliance with scheduled or promised dates. Hence, the system rates the suppliers by comparing deliveries made against scheduled or promised dates. Thus, if the supplier meets 95 percent of his quoted or promised delivery dates, he achieves an unweighted score of 95 on that factor.

Individual factor scores may be used to identify areas that need attention or to improve supplier performance where it is called for. A composite score of all three factors, however, is used as a measure of supplier total performance. The composite score may be used to identify suppliers who are improving and those who are not. It may be used to confirm longer-term patterns or trends in supplier performance. The score may also be used to allocate business shares or to screen out marginal suppliers.

The term *weighted point* means that each of the rating factors is given a specific weight or importance out of the total. If the highest score possible on combined quality, price, and delivery is 100, how much does the quality factor account for? How much does the price factor account for? How much does the delivery factor account for? As we said, these weights reflect the consensus of opinion among those customer people who are affected by supplier performance or can assess it. And the weights can be changed to reflect changing conditions or changing priorities.

To illustrate how the weighted-point system works let's assume that the customer has weighted quality at 50, net price at 25, and delivery at 25 out of a total possible score of 100.

Table 8–1 shows how quality is measured by the supplier's acceptance-rejection experience. Thus, the percentage of items or lots rejected out of the total received is weighted by a factor of 50.

Table 8-1. How quality is measured.

Drawing and Part Number	Lots Received	Lots Accepted	Lots Rejected	Percentage Accepted × Factor		Quality Control Rating
Supplier A	60	54	6	90.0	50	45
Supplier B	60	56	4	93.3	50	46.7
Supplier C	20	16	4	80.0	50	40

The customer looks at price as net price. Thus, net price—that is, unit price less discounts plus transportation charges—is weighted by a factor of 25 as shown in Table 8–2.

The customer looks at delivery as actual receipts versus scheduled or promised dates. The percentage is weighted by a factor of 25 as shown in Table 8–3.

For the composite rating, 100 is the highest score possible. Based on the particular ratings for quality, price, and delivery

Table 8–2. How price is measured.

Part A

	Unit Price – Discount ($)	(%)	+	Transportation Charge ($)	=	Net Price ($)
Supplier A	1.00	10	(.90)	.03		.93
Supplier B	1.25	15	(1.06)	.06		1.12
Supplier C	1.50	20	(1.20)	.03		1.23

Part B

	Lowest Price ($)	÷	Net Price ($)	=	Percentage	×	Factor	=	Price Rating
Supplier A	.93		.93		100		25		25
Supplier B	.93		1.12		83		25		20.8
Supplier C	.93		1.23		76		25		19.7

Table 8–3. How delivery is measured.

	Promises Kept (%)	×	Delivery Factor	=	Delivery Rating
Supplier A	90		25		22.5
Supplier B	95		25		23.8
Supplier C	100		25		25.0

shown in Tables 8–1, 8–2, and 8–3, the composite scores for Suppliers A, B, and C are shown in Table 8–4.

Point systems are rarely used as the sole basis of source selection. Rather, they are used as guides to assist in that process. For example, from the weighting factors in the example above, the customer may establish guidelines for selecting suppliers, allocating business, or identifying suppliers to be avoided. The guidelines are used by buying influences in conjunction with other supplier information or data. A typical factor evaluation guide is shown in Table 8–5.

Index Rating

With the widespread use of computers, vendor rating has progressed beyond the simple weighted-point schemes. Index rating systems evaluate supplier performance dynamically. They evaluate performance against base points of time, past performance, or other variables the customer considers relevant.

Table 8–4. Composite rating.
Part No. 67845–B

Rating	Supplier A	Supplier B	Supplier C
Quality (50 points)	45.0	46.7	40.0
Price (25 points)	25.0	20.8	20.8
Delivery (25 points)	22.5	23.8	25.0
Total Rating	92.5	91.3	85.8

Table 8–5. Factor evaluation guide.

	100 (Excellent)	94–99 (Good)	87–94 (Fair)	Under 87 (Needs Investigation —Questionable)
Quality	50	47–49	44–46	Under 44
Price	25	23–24	21–22	Under 21
Delivery	25	23–24	21–22	Under 21

Index systems enable the customer to compare current supplier quality, price, or delivery performance with that same performance six months ago, a year ago. Has it improved or remained the same? Has it deteriorated? Index systems also enable the customer to compare the performance of one supplier with another on the same purchased item, on any factor or combination of factors. Is supplier A's quality performance better than supplier B's on Part No. 3582-J? On Part No. 5782-B is supplier A's delivery performance better than B's? How much better?

The simplest rating index compares current performance with performance at a base point. For example, if the price of an item in the base year 1984 was $1.98 per unit and today it is $2.20, these facts can be shown by an index:

Base-year price: $1.98/per unit
Current price: $2.20/per unit
Relationship of the two prices: $2.20 ÷ $1.98 = 1.11

Index = 1.11 × 100 = 111

Index rating systems are used to develop such indexes for supplier price, quality, and delivery performance. As in the example above, they establish performance at the base point and relate it to current performance, then index the result. In more sophisticated systems they even factor performance for quantity or volume variations. The power of the computer to process large amounts of data rapidly makes all this possible.

Like weighted-point systems, the index system weighs each of the performance factors and reflects that weight in each factor index. The system also develops a composite index, similar in concept to the composite rating on point systems. Thus, on some specific item supplier A has a current quality index of 94, a price index of 96, and a delivery index of 98. The weights assigned to these performance factors are 50, 30, and 20 respectively. His composite index is shown in Table 8–6.

Composite Index: 9,540 ÷ 100 = 95.4

The theory behind the customer's use of weighted-point and index systems is that they reduce the subjective element in buying decisions. The reasoning is that buyers and buying influences are

Table 8-6. Index rating.

Performance Factor	Performance Factor Index		Performance Factor Weight		
Quality	94	×	50	=	4,700
Price	96	×	30	=	2,880
Delivery	98	×	20	=	1,960
			100		9,540

too reliant on memory or opinion to assess supplier performance objectively. And this is considered particularly true when they buy large numbers of items from a large number of suppliers. By accumulating factual information on rejections, delivery failures, and comparative prices and weighing them to reflect their relative importance, the customer obtains a more objective view of how suppliers perform. Or so the reasoning goes.

Both the weighted-point and index systems have some serious shortcomings. To begin with, they both evaluate supplier "price performance." The point system uses the lowest quoted price to establish the most favorable rating for price. The index system uses comparative—that is, currently quoted prices versus base point prices—for indexing. But both approaches accept a basic premise. They assume something meaningful in the notion of supplier "price performance." And that is a very questionable assumption.

Performance means action or the result of action. It is accomplishment or achievement. To combine that term with price is to imply price results, that is, prices obtained, prices paid in some past period—a price history. But for selecting suppliers, of what importance are the prices paid a year or two years ago? The important consideration is what suppliers are quoting now on the current requirement. Because these performance systems assign weights to each factor, if the weight assigned to "price performance" is high enough, it can easily obscure or distort the importance of other factors in the composite rating.

But the significant point to make is that the notion of "price performance" is not meaningful to supplier evaluation the way quality and delivery performance are. A supplier's past record in meeting scheduled or promised delivery dates is an important consideration in making a source selection. So too is the pattern of acceptances and rejections he's shown on past orders. But his past price history is not relevant. The only thing that is relevant is what price the supplier is quoting now, and whether that price is likely to result in value to the buyer.

And here is the principal weakness in most vendor rating systems. They do not look at supplier performance in terms of customer value, as we define that term. They do not view requirements, for example, as they actually exist. They view requirements only as the statistical data say they exist. And the rating systems totally ignore cost that suppliers cause in meeting or failing to meet those requirements. Misconceiving requirements and ignoring the cost of satisfying them is a sure prescription for faulty supplier evaluation.

EXAMPLE: The supplier produces to a changed specification, but the change does not appear on the drawings used in Receiving Inspection. When the item is received and inspected, it is rejected. Although the supplier expended effort and energy to make the change as the customer requested it, the system gives him an unfavorable quality rating.

EXAMPLE: The supplier is instructed to hold up shipments for a few days because of delays or bottlenecks in production. The customer's material planners do not reschedule the supplier, or the planning system cannot reschedule him until the next scheduling period. When he delivers as instructed, he is beyond the originally scheduled date. The vendor rating system gives him an unfavorable delivery rating.

EXAMPLE: Two suppliers supplying the same item are each one day late on their scheduled or promised delivery dates. When supplier A is late, it isn't even noticed because stocks of the item he supplies are ample and production rates are on the low side. When supplier B is late, however, there is a crisis. Machines are stopped; labor is idle; commitments to customers are in jeopardy. To the rating system the delivery failures are identical. The suppliers receive the same negative scores. They receive the same unfavorable rating.

These are not contrived or isolated situations. They occur every day and with increasing regularity. They occur because in the area of supplier evaluation personal experience and judgment is steadily being supplanted by computer systems and statistical measures. This is particularly true where suppliers provide production or process materials repetitively. Because there is a continuing history of transactions, the data lends itself to computer analysis. Hence, the rating systems are mathematically modeled. They are expanded and refined to include more and more statistical data. If the data is quantifiable, it is added. If not, it is ignored.

Accordingly, rating systems may pay no attention to supplier service when considering supplier performance. Supplier service is the supplier's application of capabilities to ensure the satisfaction of customer requirements, implied ones as well as those that are specified. Supplier services include:

- Technical and professional assistance in designing or specifying for customer performance, use, or application
- Support in quality improvement, product improvement, material substitution, material standardization
- Contributions to customer cost improvement in handling, packaging, and shipping
- Training of customer personnel in the operation, maintenance, and use of what he sells
- Providing of technical materials, samples, advertising literature, and marketing and financial support
- After-sale follow-up of delivery performance; the guarantee of customer satisfaction after performance occurs

Admittedly, it is difficult to quantify supplier services the way rating systems quantify quality and delivery performance. But it is not difficult to establish whether they're supplied or not. It is also not difficult to establish the quality and caliber of those services as they are supplied by competitive suppliers.

However, for services to be evaluated, buying influences must be aware that services are in fact supplied. They must know what they are, when they are supplied, the specific relationship they bear to customer requirements, the circumstances or context in which they are provided, and the results or benefits they achieve.

The buying influences must understand that supplier services contribute value in many ways:

- Supplier programs of quality improvement, value engineering, and packaging redesign reduce customer product, production, and distribution costs
- Supplier design and technical services avoid customer engineering, operating, and maintenance costs
- Supplier training of customer sales personnel, financial assistance, and advertising and marketing support offset customer cost by increasing income or improving cash flow.

These are solid and substantial contributions to customer value. But unless the customer acknowledges them, they command little or no value in exchange. The skilled salesperson, the one who understands value selling, is fully conscious of this fact. He knows his responsibilities don't end with the sale itself, or even with its successful performance or completion. He knows he must earn recognition for value supplied, and establish credibility to be a supplier of value again. He practices the advice of experienced preachers and teachers: "Tell them what you're going to tell them; tell them; and then tell them what you told them." Translated this means that the salesperson sells the customer value in the sales presentation. He takes a personal responsibility in ensuring that value is in fact supplied. He then makes sure that the customer knows and appreciates that he received the value promised.

The purchasing director for one of the companies I work with has a silver-plated sign on his desk saying: "What have you done for me lately?" Presumably, all salespeople who visit him see that sign. Whether they take it as anything more than a show of whimsy, however, I really don't know. But the question it asks is in no way whimsical. It is dead serious. And it should be taken seriously by all salespeople. The fact is, the customer's value perceptions of supplier services can be fleeting and even capricious. He appreciates those services when they are urgently needed. He is angry and feels short-changed when they are not there. But he also can take them for granted. And he even can ignore them. When this occurs the true supplier of value is penalized. And this is exactly what happens when the customer evaluates supplier performance strictly on the point scores or performance indexes of his computerized rating system.

As salespeople, we should consider the question "What have you done for me lately?" and turn it to our advantage. We should make it a regular practice to apprise the customer of value contributions we make, not only in meeting his specified requirements, but in providing services that relate to them or are implied by them. Semiannually or annually, we should submit to meaningful buying influences a report of what we have done for the customer over the period covered. The gist of such a report would be:

(1) We believe that you the customer are entitled to know what you're getting for the purchase dollars you spend with us.

(2) In addition to meeting your quality and time requirements, we have (a) expended x number of engineering or technical man-hours specifically on your account; (b) provided y dollars of marketing assistance or advertising support; (c) initiated or implemented programs for you to improve product performance, reduce manufacturing lead time, simplify order processing and handling, . . .

(3) We wish to review with you the progress of these programs, and to explore how we can serve you better in the coming year.

Customer failure to acknowledge supplier services is not universal. It is more common in customer assessments of commodity suppliers than of specialized or advanced-technology ones. A commodity is standardized, even interchangeable among all those who produce or supply it. Hence, it is easy to assume that:

- Value is solely in the supply of the commodity itself at a competitive price; and
- Service value contributions are not important or they are equal from one supplier to the next.

For these reasons computer systems are more commonly used to evaluate commodity suppliers than noncommodity ones.

On requirements that are highly specialized or one-of-a-kind, and particularly on requirements that are one-time and of high dollar value, the customer often evaluates supplier services as part of the overall supplier offering. He does so by writing them into the specifications or including them within the required work scope descriptions. For purchases of this kind, the customer acknowledges services as a defined value requirement. And suppliers sell them as part of their regular stock in trade. For example: The purchase of capital equipment demands not only consideration of the equipment's design and performance but also consideration of the services a supplier will provide over the equipment's acquisition and use life cycle. It demands:

- Technical services in its original installation
- Technical services in its preventive and corrective maintenance
- Supply services in the inventory management of its spares and repair parts
- Engineering and technical services for its documentation, including drawings, handbooks, and operating manuals
- Training services for customer personnel on its operation and maintenance, including instructors, manuals, films, and other training aids

Table 8–7 shows how bids look when the customer asks for services to be quoted as separate and distinct items of purchase.

When the customer breaks out services as line items in the requirement package, the price of the equipment itself takes on a different meaning. Note that in Table 9–6 supplier A is the

Table 8-7. Bids with services broken out.

Line Items	Supplier A	Supplier B	Supplier C
Equipment as specified	$ 42,000	$ 60,000	$ 47,000
Installation	5,000	4,000	6,000
Five-year maintenance	129,000	116,000	84,000
Five-year inventory management	45,000	30,000	42,000
New documentation	12,000	18,000	12,000
Operational training	8,000	8,000	8,000
Total Price	$241,000	$236,000	$199,000

low bidder on the equipment alone. On the equipment plus services, however, he is the high bidder. Thus, the total price is more reflective of value to the customer than the price of the equipment alone. And that is a step in the right direction.

But in breaking out services, the customer compels suppliers to be price competitive on those services just as they are on the product. And herein lies the risk both to the value seller and the value buyer. Service is not only the quantity of time expended in maintenance, documentation, and training but also the quality of that time. It is the skill and craftsmanship, the experience and judgment of those who render the services. And these are not easily assessed by dollar comparisons alone.

The credibility of a seller as a supplier of value is surely influenced by his past performance. How he produced or supplied before is a reasonable indicator of what he will do now. But in service industries and manufacturing industries of high-service content, past performance is not always a reliable indicator. Requirements differ; technical or economic considerations change. People the supplier employed before are no longer there. As a consequence, specialty and service suppliers must almost reestablish credibility with each new requirement. They must certainly reconfirm it.

Customer assessments of supplier performance rarely remain fixed. They change as product, process, or market requirements change. They change as business priorities change. A supplier whose performance was rated high on one requirement might be rated poor on another. A supplier whose performance was acceptable in a soft market might be unacceptable in a tight one. And a supplier who was a preferred source when business was good could be a poor one when cost reduction is a purchasing priority.

Within the past several years, there have been dramatic changes in the market and competitive demands imposed on American industry. The powerful inroads made by Japanese manufacturers into markets once dominated by Americans have altered radically our views of quality and assurance of supply. These are essential elements of customer requirement, so by their accomplishments the Japanese have challenged traditional notions of value to the customer. In so doing they have also challenged our views of supplier performance and our views of what makes sellers credible as suppliers of value.

One industry that has intensely felt the impact of Japanese competition is the automotive industry. And it is rapidly restructuring its processes and practices to meet the challenge. It is placing strong emphasis on computerization and robotics. The automotive industry is also standardizing design, components, and parts among its diverse model and styling mix. It is offering maintenance and warranty protections it never provided before. But probably the most far-reaching restructuring it is doing is altering its relationship with suppliers. It is changing both the size of its supply base and the criteria by which the new supply base will be evaluated.

Stated simply, the automotive industry intends to buy from considerably fewer suppliers. From the suppliers it retains, it will buy under longer-term supply agreements. The industry places the highest priority on supplier quality and will enforce quality performance rigidly. Suppliers who meet quality standards will be rewarded with new business. Those who fail will be eliminated. Although low price is an important consideration, it does not have the same significance it had before. It shares equal or comparable importance with other purchasing objectives.

In a survey of the industry's purchasing managers, the magazine *PurchasingWorld** came up with the following findings:

1. On the question of what suppliers need to supply in order to win business today, their selections and priorities were as shown in Table 8–8.
2. When asked whether these changes in requirements and priorities were permanent or temporary, the answers were: Permanent (92%), Temporary (6%), Don't Know (2%).
3. The survey asked whether by 1990 there would be more, fewer, or the same number of suppliers. The answers were: More (7%), Fewer (90%), The Same (3%). Asked to predict the percentage change in the number of suppliers, 68 percent of the respondents predicted 10 to 30 percent fewer suppliers.

---

* Reprinted with permission.

Table 8–8. What purchasing managers want from suppliers.

What Suppliers Need to Supply	First Choice (%)	Weighted for All (%)	Rank
Quality parts	81	23.1	1
Low price	7	15.5	2
Statistical process control	4	14.4	3
Engineering support	3	12.9	4
JIT (just in time) delivery	0.9	11.8	5
Yearly productivity gains	0.9	11.3	6
Innovative and/or proprietary technology	3	10.1	7
Other	—	1.2	8

As one purchasing manager put it: "They (suppliers) have got to be good . . . burn me once, and they're gone."

What's happening in the automotive industry is happening elsewhere as well. Reducing the supply base and buying to newly defined priorities is what's happening in the computer industry, electronics, the appliance industry, office equipment, telecommunications, chemicals, health care, and others. It is happening wherever supplier performance is important to customer product, process, or market demands.

The message this sends to salespeople is clear. As buying priorities change, value perceptions change. As value perceptions change, the identity and importance of buying influences change. As salespeople, we must adjust and adapt to this new selling environment. We must incorporate the value selling message in all our customer dealings—from the original sales presentation through the closing of the loop in customer satisfaction. We must establish credibility as salespeople who sell value. We must confirm and reinforce our company's credibility as a supplier of value. Anything less just will not fill the bill.

Chapter 9

NEGOTIATING FOR VALUE

The basic premise of value selling is twofold: (1) To satisfy customer requirements with cost-effectiveness and (2) to obtain value in exchange for that contribution. This is a simple concept to understand. But, when we consider its implications in day-to-day selling, the concept is difficult to apply. Consider the following:

Value to the customer is the satisfaction of customer requirements at the lowest total cost in use. That notion of value raises all kinds of questions:

Who is the customer? Or more correctly, who are the customer buying influences? What are their business or functional interests, and what are their responsibilities or areas of accountability? Are there competing or conflicting views of value among these buying influences, and how do they affect the customer's buying decisions? Obviously, the more numerous the buying influences, and the more diverse their interests and responsibilities, the more complex is the task of pinpointing who speaks for the customer and why.

What are the customer's requirements and what are the product, process, or market demands that create them? Are requirements expressly defined in specifications, bills of materials, and work scope descriptions, and are these clear, unambiguous, and fully descriptive of the customer's needs? How about the implied requirements for services and supplier capabilities the customer may not even recognize? Can they be formally acknowledged? Can they command value in exchange? If not, should they be offered or applied?

What constitutes lowest total cost in use? Is the customer's perception of cost limited solely to price and price-related factors, or is it broad enough to consider other costs of operation, maintenance, and replacement? Is the customer capable of identifying costs other than price through his existing cost-accounting system, or must he rely on estimates? Is he receptive to presentations or proposals that use cost information. Or does he assume that costs are equal with all suppliers and that price is the only significant variable?

What constitutes satisfaction of customer requirements? Is it meeting the quality, quantity, and time specifications as they are defined? Is it meeting not only defined specifications but also those that are implied in the defined specifications or implied in the buyer-seller relationship? What is truly implied by the seller and what is merely inferred by the buyer? Is it a reasonable assumption he makes or a justified conclusion he reaches when the customer infers what he does?

Value in exchange in economic theory is simply price, that is, the amount of money given for goods and services sold. In the real world of buying and selling, however, value in exchange necessarily involves factors that go way beyond that. Consider the following:

What is a reasonable price? Is it the price that competition establishes? Is it a published price? Is it published price less a competitive discount? Is it a reimbursement of cost plus a markup; reimbursement of cost plus a fee? Is it a price fixed over a contract period of time? Is it a flexible price, subject to redetermination after a specific quantity has been produced, or a specific calendar period of time has elapsed?

How is value in exchange affected by market share? Does it make a difference to the seller whether he enjoys 25 percent, 50 percent, or 100 percent of the customer's business, and is that difference reflected in price or other considerations? When we think of "other considerations," what is the value-in-exchange significance of being the customer's single-source supplier? What is the significance of having a customer commitment to buy on a multiyear rather than an as-required basis?

How is value in exchange related to profitability or to cash flow? What is the significance of price in terms of return on sale, return on assets, return on capital investment? How are these affected by product mix and by customer mix? Is the customer's business one-time or is it continuing? Are there benefits to the seller in the form of advance payments, progress payments, or prompt payment of invoices upon completion or delivery?

What are value in exchange offsets to the seller because of warranties or guarantees, liquidated damages, or penalty provisions the customer seeks? What are the probabilities of engineering changes, schedule changes, and quantity cutbacks or terminations that could alter the basis of value in exchange established in the original agreement?

When we consider these questions and the factors to which they relate, it is clear that the tasks of both buying and selling value are not easy. Indeed, effectively resolving these questions poses one of the most difficult problems facing management today.

For the salesperson, these questions of value selling pose a particularly difficult problem. The skilled salesperson acts as a catalyst, fusing the requirements of the customer with the supplier's product and service capabilities. And he fuses them so that value is supplied to the customer for value in exchange. Given the potential for controversy and conflicting interests implicit in these questions, the skilled salesperson must also be a proficient negotiator.

The term "negotiation" has entered the field of popular jargon, and in the process taken on the meaning of gamesmanship, one-upmanship, winning by ploy or intimidation. As such, negotiation becomes a hostile and contentious process in which there are winners and losers. Negotiation has also been described as a simple exercise of reaching a "win-win" agreement. The notion of "win-win" assumes that areas of dispute can be resolved so that both parties to the negotiation walk away with equal advantage. It's as if the negotiation process were like dividing a pie, with both parties getting equal portions.

In the difficult and complex environment that value sellers face, however, neither of these views of negotiation is adequate. And to the salesperson who must also be a negotiator, they present a faulty picture of what he must do and how he must act as a negotiator. Briefly, negotiation is a process of doing business (in this context, selling) through discussions, analysis, and bargaining. It is used whenever there are different objectives, interests, opinions, or points of view that must be resolved in order to reach agreement. The purpose of negotiation is to reach an agreement that is mutually acceptable, but which also satisfies one's major goals and concerns.

Thus, effective negotiation is a dual process. It is both cooperative and competitive, cooperative because it aims to broaden and refine areas of common interest and to reduce and resolve areas of controversy so that the agreement satisfies both buyer and seller alike. Negotiation is competitive because it pursues goals and interests that may differ or conflict with those of the other party.

It is this dual nature of negotiation that salespeople must understand. Selling value to the customer is a concept that demands complete involvement with the customer's needs, concerns, and constraints. It is a positive, creative process that calls for full cooperation between buyer and seller. But selling value to the customer is not an exercise in philanthropy. There are legitimate seller interests that must be protected and important seller goals that must be obtained. When these come into conflict with customer objectives, we must negotiate to resolve that conflict, and to resolve it to our advantage. Clearly, we don't jeopardize the sale or the customer relationship in pursuing that advantage. But obtaining value in exchange that is fair, reasonable, and consistent with our assessments of worth may well demand from us a competitive posture or response.

Negotiating Effectively

Consider the following real-life situations (recast with fictitious names) and decide for yourself whether they call for negotiation in the sense that we have defined that term.

EXAMPLE 1: The Calorex Company designs and builds high-temperature furnaces for manufacturing processes producing both basic and exotic materials. One year ago, Calorex sold a furnace to Transicore, which was to be built to the customer's design and performance specifications. The salesperson who made the sale was Jim Boland. He was an experienced professional and did a thorough job of establishing Transicore's requirements and what Calorex must do to meet them. The furnace was produced and delivered as scheduled, and by the customer's own admission, "it worked like a charm."

Six months later, Transicore requested Boland to submit a proposal on another furnace to be built to the "same specifications" as the first unit. The materials to be processed, however, would be totally different from those before. And Transicore would not disclose the nature or properties of those materials because of "proprietary reasons." Further, Boland had learned from Transicore's production superintendent that the production process itself would be different, involving batch rather than continuous flow.

In requesting the proposal from Calorex, Transicore expressed the opinion that no engineering charges should be included in the price, because they had already been paid for in the first furnace. They further stated that the same terms and conditions of purchase, including those on warranty and guarantee, should prevail.

Customer Objectives—to obtain the same price and the same warranty and guarantee protections on the new furnace as on the first unit.

Seller Concerns—there are risks on the second unit not present on the first. The seller's concerns are:

- To reduce the risk of increased scope of engineering and manufacturing effort because of new materials and new customer processes
- To avoid the risk of higher costs
- To minimize the risk of liability resulting from application of warranty and guarantee language applicable to the first unit but not to the second

EXAMPLE 2: Three months ago the Ransom Corporation solicited bids from four computer software firms to cover the design, development, and implementation of a management information system. Since the bid request documents were limited in scope, defining only the database, applications, and support requirements of the system, the bids were solicited on a cost-plus-fixed-fee basis. Bids were to be received in thirty days. In their proposals, the contractors were requested to submit estimates of costs, fees covering overhead and profit, their rates for systems design and programming manpower and other services, their policies concerning employee assignments, and a presentation describing their approach to managing and controlling the project. Selection of source would be by evaluating the limited cost data, along with a subjective weighing of each contractor's qualifications. The evaluations would be supported by further information and judgments obtained through a series of personal visits by Ransom's project managers to contractors' offices prior to bid submission.

All bids were received as scheduled, and within forty-five days the evaluation of proposals was completed. The contractor whose bid was evaluated most favorably was Knowlton Software. The salesperson who had found and developed the Ransom account was Harry Ferguson.

Following bid evaluation, but prior to contract award, Ferguson was asked to visit George Morris, Ransom's vice-president of finance. The meeting was cordial but disturbing. Morris told Ferguson that because of falling sales and the need to hold costs down wherever possible, Ransom had to reconsider the entire project. There was no question that Ransom badly needed the information system, and that Knowlton was the best-qualified source to develop it. But facts were facts. Unless Knowlton agreed to convert its bid into a not-to-exceed fixed price, Ransom would be forced to postpone the project until economic conditions improved.

Customer Objectives—to limit and control costs of the system by converting a cost-plus-fee proposal into a not-to-exceed fixed price.

Seller Concerns—The economic, management and other considerations reflected in a not-to-exceed fixed price proposal are not the same as those for a cost-plus-fee one. There is substantial exposure to cost overruns, which are at the seller's expense. There is risk of being tied down in reprogramming and debugging, again at seller expense. The seller's concerns, therefore, are:

- To avoid committing on the basis of a pricing formulation that is not only dangerous, but also contrary to the original price proposal
- To keep the business already "sold"
- To avoid any delays in the project

EXAMPLE 3: The Cortland Electric Company agreed to buy an estimated 180,000 power relays over an eighteen-month period from Gary Electronics. The relays were to be produced to Cortland's specifications, and delivery would be on an "as-released" basis. Because of unexpected increases in demand that Cortland experienced on an earlier purchase from Gary, Dave Lewis, Cortland's purchasing manager, instructed Ernie Watts, Gary's sales engineer, to "manufacture sufficiently in advance, so that you can meet our needs without interruption."

Through purchase order releases, Cortland scheduled the relays for delivery at the rate of 10,000 per month for the first six months. It then increased the rate to 15,000 per month for the following six months. In the twelfth month of the agreement, Cortland instructed Gary to reduce the rate of delivery to 5,000 per month for the next three months, and to make no more units until Cortland issued specific instructions to that effect. In the fifteenth month of the agreement, Lewis telephoned Watts and told him that because of falling demand there were no further requirements for the relays and that Gary should make no further shipments until Cortland assessed its inventory position.

From the time of its original agreement with Cortland two years before, Gary had always produced the relays in batches of 60,000 because of the special processing required and the high setup and start-up costs that involved. At a delivery rate of 10,000 per month, this was a six-month supply, and at a delivery rate of 15,000 per month, it was a four-month supply. In either event, the quantities produced would well ensure the continuous and uninterrupted supply that Cortland required. At the time of Lewis's call to Watts, Gary had 45,000 completed units on hand and raw materials sufficient for an additional 30,000 units.

Customer Objective—to take no further units and to limit its obligations under the agreement.

Seller Concerns

- To achieve compliance with the agreement or obtain full reimbursement for costs incurred, plus profit
- To retain Cortland as a customer for future business

EXAMPLE 4: Norton Chemicals entered into a lump-sum contract with the Bellows Company for the construction of an addition to their Cumberland plant. Bellows in turn subcontracted a portion of the structural work to R & H Construction.

One of the requirements in the R & H contract was for the subcontractor to install large sections of stainless steel piping in the ground. The piping was to be in thirty-six-foot lengths, welded without seams, and certified as to chemical and physical property.

As a result of a routine inspection by Norton field personnel, it was discovered that one thirty-six-foot length of the final section of piping installed was welded to that length out of nine four-foot lengths. As a consequence, Norton insisted that all the pipe now installed be excavated, inspected, and replaced where necessary with seamless pipe as specified. Only one thirty-six-foot length of pipe was found sectionally welded. Although the pipe was obtained from more than one supplier, there was no evidence to conclude that the rest of the pipe was not according to specification. But there was also no evidence to the contrary.

When the subcontractor, R & H, was told of Norton's demand, his reaction was: "If I am forced to make this replacement, I've got to pull a crew off another part of this project, which means a delay on that portion of the work." To hire an outside piping contractor so that the job would not be held up would mean added cost coming out of Bellow's pocket.

As Jim Billotti, Bellows's vice-president of sales, considered the problem, he asked himself: "How the hell do I pull all these pieces together?"

Customer Objectives

- To excavate, inspect, and replace where necessary all pipe now installed that does not conform to specification. Actually, the customer's objective—although not stated—is to gain assurance that all piping now installed meets specification. A somewhat different objective!
- To incur no additional cost

Seller Concerns

- To provide assurance to the customer that the pipe does meet specifications; to replace it where it doesn't at minimum cost to Bellows
- To do so with no interruptions or delays
- To satisfy the customer that his requirements will be met and that Bellows is a responsible supplier

EXAMPLE 5: Recently, the Newmark Company decided to purchase all of its corrugated containers under long-term agreements. Under these agreements, Newmark would estimate its total annual usage, by size and by types of construction. From these estimates, Newmark would contract with a supplier for specific quantities and deliveries as they were needed. The reasoning was that this would greatly reduce the time and paper work involved in buying the containers. And more important, it should generate significant cost savings.

Newmark's buyer of packaging materials was Julie Britt. Britt was new to Newmark, but had had ten to twelve years' buying experience at two military electronics companies. She prided herself on knowing packaging materials and on knowing container construction. She even developed rough estimates of what she thought the container should cost in terms of paperboard and liner materials, as well as container processing time.

Britt invited quotations from six approved suppliers, on both a unit price basis and in terms of a total dollar price for all sizes and quantities. She indicated to suppliers that she would screen out the least-competitive ones and "discuss" her requirements further with the one or two whose quotations were most attractive.

Accordingly, Britt notified the Rabin Paper Company that she was "seriously considering" their proposal. She asked that Dave Minott, Rabin's sales representative, come in to talk with her. When Minott sat down at Britt's desk, he was told that Rabin's quotations were generally "in the ball park" but that on several container sizes they were "not in line." However, she said that in order to make a "meaningful" evaluation as to how reasonable the quotations really were, she wanted a breakdown of the price. Specifically, she asked Minott to supply her with the cost allowances built into Rabin's prices for materials, labor, overhead, and profit.

Customer Objective—clearly and without any doubt, to drive Rabin's prices down

Seller Objectives—to fulfill his responsibility of supplying value to the customer for reasonable value in exchange. The seller's cost is not a significant factor of value to the customer. Value is satisfying the customer's requirements at the lowest total cost to him. It is cost to the customer that is important, not cost to the seller. Further, the competitive process, which Rabin successfully met, is the customer's own criterion for source selection. Hence, the competitive price is a reasonable expression of reasonable value in exchange.

The situations described are not theoretical or out of the ordinary. They are real, they are common, and they occur every day. And they highlight the fact that implicit in the acts of buying and selling are differences in objectives, interests, and concerns. These differences are present regardless of personal attitude or intentions, even though both parties wish to reach agreement. Obviously once an agreement is reached, those differences will be resolved. But objectively, they will be resolved to one or the other's advantage. Your aims, therefore, should be:

1. To reach an agreement that provides objective advantage
2. To reach an agreement that is acceptable and satisfying to the customer

You achieve those aims by negotiating for them. Negotiation is a continual process vital to successful value selling. It begins with the first contacts with customer buying influences and continues through the sales presentation, the closing of the sale, and the after-sale follow-up. Negotiation takes place on matters of specifications, delivery or completion dates, prices, and terms and conditions of sale. It takes place on matters of specification changes, product or service performance, and responsibilities and liabilities that flow from these. The salesperson does not negotiate with customer buying influences only. He is often required to do so with his own management or operating people who perform, produce, or supply what the customer requires. Indeed, without negotiation, the selling of value is a practical impossibility.

Earlier in this chapter, successful negotiation was described as a dual process that is at once cooperative and competitive. This is a difficult enough concept to grasp in theory. It is infinitely more difficult to apply in practice. Yet, for salespeople to be effective negotiators, they must not only understand this dichotomy; they must implement it. And to implement it demands an attitude that is attuned and conditioned to the process. For many of us, this can pose a serious problem because, whether we are aware of it or not, we are intimidated by negotiation.

Much of the popular literature on "how to negotiate" proceeds from the basic assumption that anyone can negotiate. All that is required to negotiate successfully is to size up the adversary's psychological and emotional weak points, master some tactics and ploys, and presto, you've got your man just where you want him. Sad—or perhaps happy—to say, nothing could be further from the truth.

To begin with, not everyone can or will negotiate. Many of us are inhibited by the negotiation process. By its very nature negotiation involves controversy, if not conflict. And that means that by negotiating we could wind up on the losing end of the stick, or suffer the pain of having our egos bruised. With those risks, we do not go out of our way to invite or promote the negotiation process.

Beyond the threat we perceive to our well-being or self-esteem, we are inhibited by negotiation because of our cultural conditioning. The images our media convey of negotiation are those of haggling, dickering, doing business in a bazaarlike fashion. Negotiation is not nice. It's not American. It's foreign, ill-mannered, or crude. And given these views, we are not comfortable in the negotiating process.

Again, our cultural conditioning does not encourage and reinforce the essential requirement for successful negotiation, namely, the conscious and continuing sense of self-interest. The relative affluence of our society may account for that. If we had to worry from one day to another where our next meal was coming from, we would be more acutely aware of our self-interest and how to pursue it. But in our society, pursuit of self-interest is easily seen as selfishness. And selfishness is antisocial, so negotiating to pursue self-interest becomes exploitative. And that can be seen as unprofessional, if not unethical.

Given these media, cultural, and societal perceptions, it is not surprising that many of us are inhibited by the negotiation process. But the critical fact that sales people must understand is that to sell value to the customer for acceptable value in exchange, we must negotiate. No matter how close and cooperative the relationship between buyer and seller may be, they and we view our dealings from different perspectives.

• Specifications, which at first glance may appear clear and unambiguous, are still subject to different interpretations. What is a "clean surface"? What is "good operating condition"? What is "reasonable performance"? What is the meaning of "painted white"? An EPA requirement for materials is that they be "aesthetically pleasing."

• Quantities for which suppliers are asked to quote can mean different things to different people. Are the quantities to be firmly committed? Are they only estimates or forecasts? Do they reflect actual past usage or merely projections of usage? How are quantities related to rates of delivery, as now scheduled or as released?

• Price is the amount of money that changes hands between buyer and seller. What is a reasonable price? How will it be determined? How will it take into consideration the following price-related factors?

—The risks of unanticipated changes in work scope
—The risks of cancellation
—The risks of strikes, machine breakdowns, supplier delays
—The risks of escalating costs over the contract life

And when we consider the differences in buyer-seller perspective on what constitutes "responsible performance" in fulfilling contractual obligations, the need to negotiate should be even more obvious. What is the meaning of contract language that says:

• *"Seller shall implement all changes that Buyer directs in a timely and expeditious manner."* What is a "timely and expeditious manner"?
• *"Within reason, the Seller shall meet the Buyer's delivery requirements by arranging the Seller's material and production schedules in anticipation of Buyer's needs."* What is "within reason" in "anticipation of Buyer's needs"?
• *"If any of the goods are found at any time to be defective, Buyer shall have the right to reject and return such goods at Seller's expense."* What is the meaning of "at any time"? Is it forever? How is it established whether items rejected are truly "defective"? If goods are rejected and returned, what are the "expenses" the Seller is liable for?

The need to negotiate is pervasive. And it is for this reason that salespeople must develop a positive attitude toward the process. If you do not invite or promote negotiation, you cannot successfully sell value. Surely, you cannot command acceptable value in exchange.

The first step in developing a positive attitude is to recognize your own inhibitions toward negotiation, and then to overcome them. This begins with recognizing the need to negotiate. Once you acknowledge the need to negotiate, your inhibitions begin to fade.

It is only after losing your inhibitions that you can really develop negotiating skills. No matter how many books you read or video tapes you see about the negotiating process, you will not be an effective negotiator in practice until you are positively disposed to the process. You must believe it's necessary and be confident in what it can do. When you are mentally and emotionally attuned to negotiation as a basic instrument for value selling, you can then develop the knowledge and skills of its practice.

I have dwelt on this point because it is a matter about which I have strong feelings. In more than thirty years of training and consulting experience, I have seen all kinds of money and time expended on "negotiation" training. All too often, these efforts jump into the "how to's" of negotiating, with little or no consideration of a rationale for negotiation. Why do we negotiate? When do we negotiate? Are there social, ethical, or psychological factors that inhibit us from negotiating? It has been my experience that if an acceptable rationale for negotiation is not provided, those who are "trained" to negotiate will not do so. They may be intellectually stimulated by the subject. They may find the training exercises exciting and even fun. But they will not use in practice what they have "learned." Learning means that the learner changes his ways of doing things, or changes his perceptions of things. And if one's attitude toward negotiation remains inhibited, he has not truly learned to negotiate.

Developing a Negotiation Strategy

The word *strategy* comes from the ancient Greek *strategia*, which means "office of the general." And even in its modern usage, the word maintains its military connotations. Thus, the dictionary defines *strategy* as the "science or art of military command as applied to overall planning and conduct of large scale combat operations." A more colloquial definition calls *strategy* the "art or skill of using stratagems in politics, business, courtship, or the like." But a *stratagem* is still defined as a "military maneuver designed to deceive or surprise an enemy." Hence, a strategy is employed in a confrontation with an adversary over objectives that may be won or lost through strengths and weaknesses, depending on how skillfully or poorly they are used.

Successful negotiation in value selling requires a negotiation strategy because one of the dual facets of negotiation is competitiveness. And whenever there is competition there is confrontation with an adversary over objectives. Unfortunately, the word *adversary* conjures up the image of an enemy to be defeated, and in all fairness, there are certainly situations where this is precisely the case. But in a value selling scenario, the customer is an "adversary" only because on specific issues his goals and interests are different from our own. And to resolve those differences we negotiate.

A negotiating strategy is an all-encompassing plan for action. We develop a strategy to:

- Determine areas of agreement and disagreement
- Evaluate the resources of people, time, and information we need to negotiate successfully
- Develop the course of action we will follow in the negotiation itself

The strategy performs the following four specific functions:

1. It identifies negotiation objectives—both the customer's and our own—in some known or likely order of priority.
2. It identifies negotiation issues, that is, matters that are in dispute, ambiguous, or subject to different interpretation or opinion.
3. It assesses respective strengths and weaknesses as they pertain to buyer-seller objectives and interests.

4. From these identifications and assessments, it lays out an action plan.

Setting objectives is the crucial first step in developing an effective negotiation strategy. Yet, it is astonishing how little attention is given to this task. Time and again, I have seen otherwise responsible people—managers, salespeople, purchasing agents—enter into negotiations without having thought out fully what they want to get and what they're willing to give up in the negotiation. They'll see "how the ball bounces," they'll "play it by ear"—two very sure prescriptions for failure!

Setting objectives means identifying those goals or advantages you wish to obtain, those interests you wish to protect or pursue. Obviously, objectives or interests that are not in dispute or which are already matters of agreement are not negotiation objectives. They are factors that can influence the negotiation, but they are not negotiation objectives themselves.

For the salesperson, negotiation objectives may be:

- Looser, broader, less restrictively defined specifications
- Firmer commitments for customer quantities or delivery schedules
- Less constraining completion dates or performance times
- Higher prices or price indexing
- More favorable terms and conditions of sale—guarantees, terminations, etc.
- More favorable terms of payment

For the customer the objectives may be merely mirror images of our own. He wants specifications as defined. He seeks to avoid commitments. He needs firm completion or delivery dates. He looks for lower prices and fixed prices. And he wants to buy under his terms and conditions of purchase, at terms of payment favorable to him.

Thus, the exercise of identifying objectives is also an exercise in identifying negotiating issues. Issues are matters that are in dispute or matters that remain unresolved. They are the substantive considerations that drive the negotiation.

Many issues, such as differences over specifications, completion dates, or price are easy to identify. But others are more subtle, and even contrived.

Indeed, one of the serious risks to the negotiator who does little or no strategy planning is that he is vulnerable to contrived issues raised by his adversary in the negotiation itself. Not having done his homework beforehand, he can't easily distinguish between a real issue and a contrived one. This forces him to address both, with the danger of making concessions on both.

The Value Selling Checklist in Chapter 5 (Table 5–1) identifies a whole range of factors that are potential objectives and issues in any specific negotiation. You should review that checklist, and then list in detail those objectives and interests that are important to you. Be as clear and specific as you can in identifying them. If it is a price objective, quantify it. Better still, quantify it and bracket it. What is the highest price you can hope for? What is the lowest price you will accept? What is the likely price you can agree on? If it is a delivery objective, do the same thing. What is the delivery schedule that best suits your production, inventory, or cost concerns? What delivery schedule can you only "live with"? What is a reasonable schedule you can compromise on?

Clearly, not all objectives you identify will have the same importance. So after you identify them, you should rank them in order of importance. Preferably, you should weight each objective by its relative importance to other objectives. For example, out of a total weight of one hundred, how much weight do you give the importance of your specification objective? Your price objective? Your terms and conditions of sale objective? By identifying and weighting each objective, you get a clearer picture of what you want to accomplish in the negotiation and a basis for allocating your resources in doing so.

Identifying and weighting objectives is the first part of the negotiation strategy process. The second part is identifying and weighting the objectives of the other party. Here you begin from the requirements the customer has expressly defined in his specifications, bills of materials, work scope descriptions, quantity and time schedules, completion dates, and so on. You should also identify objectives that are implied in his specifications or in the customer-seller relationship. It may well be that the customer doesn't even acknowledge such objectives. But if in your opinion he ought to acknowledge them, identify them. Such objectives could become bargaining issues in the actual negotiations that follow.

From whatever sources of information you have concerning the customer—his needs, his wants, his technical and business concerns—identify any other objectives you think he may have. As in identifying your own, you must be clear and precise in defining what you understand as a customer objective. If possible, quantify it, bracket it. What is the highest price you think he'll pay? What's the lowest price he could reasonably expect to pay? What is a likely price he can agree to? Again, you should weight these objectives in terms of what you think their relative importance is to the customer. If quality assurance is his primary objective, how does it compare against his price objective? Is it twice as important or only 10 percent more important?

Identifying objectives—the customer's and your own—serves two very important purposes of value selling:

1. **It identifies those areas that are common areas of interest, purpose, and concern.** Negotiation is a cooperative process that demands mutual respect, understanding, and intention to agree. The larger and broader those common areas are, or can be made to be, the stronger the likelihood of agreement is. The more compatible the notions of value to the customer are with our own, the more successful the negotiation will be.

2. **It identifies areas that are unresolved or in dispute.** That is, it identifies negotiation issues. Negotiation, as we said, is also a competitive process in which you seek to resolve issues to your advantage. If you have weighed the importance of objectives to both the customer and yourself, you have simplified the task of resolving issues. For example, the customer's objective on quantities and rates of delivery may not be too much in conflict with your objective for more favorable production rates. With a little creative problem solving you may be able to satisfy his quantity and delivery goals and still achieve the advantages of economical quantity runs. On the other hand, the customer's and your own price objectives may not be so easy to resolve. Here the differences may be major ones, so price will be an issue throughout the negotiation process. As a value seller, you know that

supplying value to the customer demands a reasonable value in exchange. And in the competitive arena of the negotiating process, that becomes a major negotiating objective.

All competitive situations are contests of power. The relative strength or weakness of the contestants determines the outcome. The winner is the one who runs the fastest, jumps the highest, or covers the course in the fewest strokes. And that fact is no different in the competitive environment of negotiation. The parties who come to the negotiating table bring to that table strengths and weaknesses, which influence not only the issues they discuss but also the resolution of those issues. Who gains objective advantage in the encounter is determined in large measure by the question of power. Who has it? Who doesn't?

Earlier we made the point that many of us are inhibited by negotiation. And one source of that inhibition is our reluctance to face up to the competitive facet of negotiation and the importance of power it implies. To acknowledge competition means to acknowledge a challenge in which someone wins and someone loses. It may be comforting to talk about "win-win" negotiation. But the facts are that in terms of objective concessions given and gained, all negotiations involve the risk of loss. And the fear of loss is a powerful motivating force. It strongly inhibits attitudes and actions. It encourages rationalizing that if we are not assertive in pursuing our objectives, our adversary won't be either. And that should reduce the risk of both our substantive and psychic loss.

Even if we acknowledge the competitive side of negotiation, we can still be inhibited by the process. The willingness to compete implies a commitment to use the means or power to compete successfully. One does not accept the challenge to a physical contest if unprepared to use the skills he has to compete. And one cannot negotiate if he doesn't use his strengths and capitalize on his adversary's weaknesses to advantage. In brief, to negotiate successfully we must use power. And that to some of us is the source of guilt or ethical concern, both of which feelings are strongly inhibiting.

Power is the ability or capacity to perform effectively. It is the capability or resources that can be used to achieve results. Power is the essential element of strength and weakness. If power is there and we have the will to employ it, that is a source of strength. If power is not there, or we are unwilling to employ it, that is a source of weakness.

Power in itself is neither morally good nor bad. It is a fact; it is a reality. And the use of power is not a moral issue, unless our objectives in using it involve moral questions. If I use power to take what belongs to another or to cause injury to someone else, my objective is immoral and my use of power is wrong. But if I use power to perform effectively a valid and necessary function, the question of morality and power is not relevant. Does anyone challenge on moral grounds the use of power to feed the hungry, cure the sick, maintain the peace? Of course not! The objectives of power in those instances are morally good, so it is the objectives of power that create the moral question, not the use of power itself. Indeed, there may well be a moral question in not using the power we have, and thereby not achieving a valid and necessary objective.

Negotiating to sell value to the customer for reasonable value in exchange is a valid and necessary business objective. And using power to achieve it is a correct and acceptable use of power. Salespeople should have no qualms about developing a strategy based on power and no sense of guilt about implementing it.

A successful negotiating strategy considers the factor of power in assessing buyer and seller strengths and weaknesses on negotiating issues. Issues are matters that are in dispute or unresolved. And we identify them by first identifying our own and the customer's objectives, interests, and concerns. Those that are yet to be agreed upon are negotiating issues. And the power we have to resolve them to our advantage is a source of our negotiating strength.

Power derives from many sources, some of which are accidental. Others are planned and promoted. Some are external to the negotiators and in no way influenced by personal considerations. Others are purely personal. Following are some of the more important sources of power that determine buyer and seller strengths and weaknesses.

1. **General and specific economic conditions.** A source of power to buyer and seller alike are general and specific economic conditions. No matter what the issue, the negotiating positions of buyer

and seller are affected by the state of the economy as a whole, and even more so by the state of the economy in their respective industries. If business is booming, with backlogs climbing and sales exceeding forecasts, the seller's negotiating position is strong. On the other hand, if business is weak, with sales declining and prices eroding steadily, the seller's negotiating position is weak. This is a circumstance well beyond the ability of either buyer or seller to affect. But it is a fact that both must live with, and it is a fact that influences the negotiation's outcome.

2. **Competition.** The existence of competition is a source of power. The more active and aggressive that competition is, the stronger the buyer's negotiating position is. Conversely, the more the buyer is forced to deal with a single supplier, the weaker his negotiating position is. And this is true not only in terms of the overall negotiation but also in terms of specific issues. Obviously, the more the competitive factor bears directly on a negotiating issue, the greater its competitive impact will be. Thus, the price issue immediately reflects competition—the more competitive the situation, the stronger the buyer's position on the price issue; the less competitive the situation, the stronger the seller's position.

3. **Uniqueness or exclusivity of the seller's offering.** Uniqueness or exclusivity of an offering may in fact preclude competition. But even if it doesn't, the fact that what the seller supplies is different from what others supply is a source of power (assuming of course that it still satisfies the customer's requirements). The uniqueness may be real or merely perceived. It is real when there are objective differences in design, performance, or reliability of the product; when it is patented or contains proprietary features. Uniqueness or exclusivity may also be perceived by those who specify or use what the seller supplies. This is an important reason for establishing and maintaining credibility with the customer. It becomes a source of power and strength in one's negotiating position.

4. **Ability to satisfy or deny; ability to help or hurt.** A source of power is the ability of both buyer and seller to satisfy or deny the needs or desires of the other, to help or hurt the other. The more dependent the seller is on the buyer for new business, higher prices, less stringent interpretation of specifications, the stronger the buyer's negotiating position is. The more the buyer depends on the seller for quality assurance, uninterrupted supply, timely delivery or completion, the stronger the seller's negotiating position is. Implicit in the buying-selling relationship is the potential for both benefit and harm, reward

and punishment. The more critical these factors are and the more capable the buyer or seller is to affect the other's well-being, the stronger his negotiating position is.

5. **Information.** Information is an important source of power. The more we know about what we sell, what the customer's requirements are, what the customer's costs are, the stronger our negotiating position is. Similarly, the more the customer knows about what we sell, how it's produced, what it costs to produce, the stronger his negotiating position is. The more information we have about who customer buying influences are; what objectives and interests they pursue; the nature and scope of their policies, systems, and practices; the use they make of what we supply, the stronger our negotiating position is. Knowing the customer in depth and keeping informed at all times of what affects him is a source of power in the negotiating process.

6. **Time.** Time is a totally impersonal factor, capable of working to buyer or seller advantage. As such, time is a source of power. At the risk of oversimplifying, the essence of negotiating strength is the ability to hold out, to avoid conceding. And time is an important factor that impinges on that ability. Who needs to reach agreement quickly, the buyer or seller? For whom is the clock running faster, the buyer or seller? One of the serious weaknesses of customer computerized scheduling systems is that they ignore the realities of the negotiation process. Thus, they schedule production on the basis of supplier "lead times" (delivery times) that assume a fixed number of days from the determination of requirements to actual delivery. If an order is not placed with a supplier within the time allowed, delivery will be late and production will suffer. As a consequence, the purchasing agent has little latitude to negotiate. Time is running against him. On the other hand, if the buyer's requirements are discretionary, if he can delay or postpone the purchase indefinitely, time is running against the seller. Time can be comforting or cruel, but it is always a source of power in negotiation.

7. **Correctness of one's position.** Although negotiators pursue different goals and interests and express different opinions or points of view, there are objective criteria that apply to their respective positions. These criteria are technical, legal, and economic principles and ethical standards or norms. The fact that one's position conforms to such criteria is a source of power. For example:

- The buyer contends that the seller's product does not meet physical or performance specifications. Test results, laboratory certifications, and physical or chemical analysis can establish the fact.

- The buyer asserts that costs he incurs to correct claimed seller defects are rightful charges against the seller. Whose terms and conditions obtain, and what does the contract say? If the contract language is silent or unclear, what is the law?
- The buyer seeks a price that is lower than the competitive price or lower than the seller's actual costs. If the buyer induces the seller to sell below the competitive price, that may be illegal. If the buyer seeks a price below actual seller cost, that may be poor economics and unreasonable.

In negotiation, virtue is more than its own reward. The correctness of one's position is a source of power, and an element of strength in the negotiating process.

8. **Precedents, conventions, customs.** A source of power that applies to buyer and seller alike is the existence of precedents, conventions, or customs. The way things have been done before, and the way situations have been resolved before influence their resolution now. There is an element of legitimacy that attaches to past practice, and this can work to the buyer's or seller's advantage. For example:

- It is a source of power for the buyer to claim that "it has always been our policy to have at least two active sources on every major item of purchase."
- It is a source of power for the seller to assert that his proposal conforms to the technical standards or recommended contract language of a technical or professional society, a contractor's association, or the "practice of the trade."

It is interesting how we can be intimidated by the thought of breaking with convention. And it is surprising how a negotiating position can be strengthened or weakened by a reference to past practice or precedent. One is easily put on the defensive when confronted with the fact that "this is not what you did before."

9. **Recourse to higher authority.** Another source of power is one's ability to reach a higher authority than those with whom he negotiates. If you have access to your adversary's superiors, with the likelihood of a more sympathetic hearing from them, that is a source of power to you. Similarly, if your adversary can go over your head or bypass you completely to resolve your differences, that is a source of power for him. It is for this reason that salespeople who enter into important negotiations must be sure that all parties who can influence

the outcome—particularly superiors and functional peers—be in full accord on negotiating objectives, strategies, and tactics, and that they reinforce the salesperson's position rather than undermine it.

10. **Sense of obligation or duty.** It is a source of power for one party to a negotiation when his adversary is forced by a sense of obligation or duty to follow or avoid any particular course of action. The strong desire to pay back past debts or reciprocate past favors reduces self-interest and self-assertiveness. The need to conform to perceived norms of acceptable conduct, behavior, or business practice reduces risk taking and aggressiveness. And these in turn reduce negotiating leverage. Buyers in large, publicly owned companies or in government agencies are often at a negotiating disadvantage because of their concern about the image they might convey by bold or unorthodox tactics. Indeed, under these circumstances even weakness can become a source of negotiating strength. I have seen many instances where large companies have literally surrendered to the demands of small or weak suppliers. Out of fear of jeopardizing that "public image," they have excused shoddy workmanship, condoned delivery delinquency, and agreed to prices they would not accept from larger or stronger suppliers. And this points out another important reason for salespeople to know the customer in depth: By knowing his policies, practices, buying philosophy, and sense of ethics, you strengthen your negotiating position.

11. **Expectations.** The expectations the buyer and seller bring to the negotiating table are a source of power. Negotiation seeks advantage, but with mutual satisfaction. And it is this interplay between advantage and satisfaction that makes expectations an element of strength or weakness. If the advantage you hope to gain from negotiation is small, it will take only small concessions to satisfy you. You will also be prepared to make concessions of your own as the situation demands them. If, on the other hand, your expectations of advantage are large, you will look for more and larger concessions from your adversary. You will make fewer and smaller concessions of your own.

It has been my experience that the higher the expectations you carry to the negotiating process, the greater the advantage you gain. There is one important caveat, however. Expectations must be realistic. They must be attainable. They must be within the bounds of reasonableness. If they are extreme, exaggerated, or unreasonable, they will be resisted, ignored, or even ridiculed. And when this occurs, power moves to the adversary.

12. **Personal attitudes and skills.** Negotiation is a highly personal process. Therefore, personal attitudes and skills become a source of

power or weakness. We know that some of us can be inhibited by negotiation. And, clearly, that is an attitude that makes for weakness. To be successful as negotiators, we must be positive, confident, and optimistic that what we pursue we will attain. The more sincere and assured we are in expressing that attitude, the stronger our negotiating position becomes. What is true of our attitude is equally true of our skills. How effectively we listen, how clearly we communicate, how we analyze problems and how creatively we solve them, how well we persuade and motivate others, and how we control our own emotions are all vital to the negotiation's outcome. These are the skills of negotiation, and how they are employed determines strength or weakness in a negotiating position.

Now that we understand the sources of power, we can go back and address in better detail the planning of negotiation strategy. Power is what makes for strength or weakness in a negotiating position. And a well-planned strategy assesses strength or weakness on objectives and issues.

Using the Value Selling Checklist shown in Table 5–1, together with the customer's defined and implied requirements and other information as guides, identify your and the customer's objectives, interests, and concerns that are in dispute or unresolved. These are the negotiating issues.

Negotiation Strategy Worksheet

On the left side of a sheet of paper list these issues in their order of importance. For greater clarity, weight them. Out of a total score of 100, how much does the first issue warrant? The second? . . .

Across the top of the page, list the customer buying influences who will be involved in the negotiation and then list yourself. Under each buying influence and yourself, set up two pairs of columns for checking factors critical to your strategy. The first deals with the matter of how strongly the customer and you feel about the negotiation issues. How strongly is each committed to gaining advantage on them? In terms of degree of commitment to the issue, classify your respective intentions as:

M Must have
L Would like to have
I Are indifferent about

The second set of columns deals with relative strengths and weaknesses in negotiating over these issues. How much power does each of us have to pursue and gain advantage on them? Classify this factor as:

S A strong position
W A weak position
N Neither a strong nor weak position—neutral

Table 9–1 is a sample negotiation strategy worksheet.

In formulating a negotiating strategy, you should strive for accuracy. But assessing respective strengths and weaknesses is difficult. And assessing your adversary's actual intentions or expectations is at best an estimate. You're considering matters that are largely conjectural. You can only speculate, or make educated judgments as to what they really are. Nonetheless, it is important that you go through the exercise of assessing and evaluating these factors to the best of your ability. Such assessments become the basis of your negotiating position and your strategy action plans.

A negotiating position is a program of benefits we want out of a negotiation in some meaningful order of importance. What we want may be a specific objective, such as the price we proposed. It may be an interest we seek to gain or protect, such as to become or remain the principal supplier to the customer. It may be a particular definition of specification or contract language. Or perhaps it is the assurance that we will be given the opportunity to meet competitive quotations.

An action plan in a negotiation strategy identifies primary, secondary, and discretionary goals in a negotiating position and considers how to pursue them. It identifies similar goals in an adversary's position as you believe he'll pursue them. The action plan also provides for a fallback or alternative position that you can take if actual negotiation makes that necessary. And it estimates what that fallback or alternative position might be for your adversary as well.

Table 9–1. Negotiation strategy worksheet.

Negotiating Issues	Customer Project Manager						Customer Purchasing Manager						Us					
	Commitment			Strength/Weakness			Commitment			Strength/Weakness			Commitment			Strength/Weakness		
	M	L	I	S	W	N	M	L	I	S	W	N	M	L	I	S	W	N
1) Customer has asked us to implement new process controls to ensure quality. We believe our current quality levels are higher than those actually specified. We also do not want to incur additional—and to us—unnecessary costs.	X					X	X				X		X				X	
2) Customer has asked for quantity and delivery as determined by actual requirements. We want a firm and definite schedule now.		X				X	X				X		X				X	
3) Customer has indicated that because it is a repeat purchase, a price reduction is "in order." Our price is competitive. Further, costs of materials and labor have gone up. We want to give no price concession.		X			X		X				X		X				X	
4) Customer wants to buy on his purchase order terms. We want our terms and conditions of sale.	X			X			X			X					X			X

5) Customer wants to maintain a three-month inventory at all times at no additional cost to him. We say if he wants it he has to pay for it.

6)

7)

8)

9)

10)

Like a military strategy, a negotiation strategy requires logistical support to be implemented effectively. It requires the allocation of people, time, skills, and techniques. And it requires that these be tailored and adapted to the specific demands of each negotiation. To be specific:

Do the nature and issues of the negotiation call for the salesperson to negotiate alone, or do they demand a team approach? If there should preferably be a team negotiation, who ought to be members of the team? Should they have strong technical or professional backgrounds or should they be financial specialists or operating managers? Who should be the team leader? Does he have the knowledge, experience, and acceptance to be an effective team leader? Should the team include higher management? If so, should they participate in the negotiation from the very beginning, or should they come in later?

When should negotiations start? How long should they last? Do we have that much time available to spend on negotiation, in view of other demands on our time? Does the customer? Which of us has more flexibility to see the negotiation through? Are there preliminary matters that must be addressed before negotiation can begin in earnest? How long will they take and what will that do to our flexibility? What will it do to the customer's? What happens in the event of a deadlock?

Where should the negotiations take place? There are pluses and minuses no matter where they occur. The customer has a psychological advantage if he negotiates on his own home grounds. However, he also has the disadvantage insomuch as he can be distracted, interrupted, or sidetracked by his other responsibilities. He also cannot easily demand that we supply additional information when that is back in our office, plant, or laboratory.

What information must we have to negotiate effectively? Should we have reports on past delivery and quality performance; information on work in process, stage of its completion, and expected delivery dates? Should we supply data on engineering, technical, and professional services we rendered over and above those specified? What negotiation techniques should we employ and what are those that the customer is likely to use? Will he discuss price in terms of our costs to produce? Will he analyze prices in terms of past prices paid, in terms of cost indexes or indicators? Will he do milestone or critical path analysis of our delivery or performance proposals? Can we do similar analyses and will they support our position?

What skills are most important to the success of the negotiation, given the issues to be negotiated and whom we will negotiate with? Is it skill in listening, analyzing, thinking logically and clearly? Is it skill in abstract thinking and communicating creative and imaginative compromises? Do we have these skills and do we employ them well? If we don't have them, can we develop them? When and how?

The goal of successful negotiation is objective advantage with mutual satisfaction. This is always a difficult and delicate task to achieve. It demands from the negotiator full attention to what he wants and how he goes about pursuing it. It also demands that he be constantly aware of what the customer wants, and how the customer pursues those wants. And compounding the problem, the negotiator must be sufficiently detached from the process to determine as objectively as he can the negotiation's progress. Who has gained a point? Who has lost a point? Whose negotiating position is weakening or beginning to erode? To be both an effective participant and a detached observer in the dynamics of a negotiating give-and-take would be impossible without a strategy. And for this reason negotiators must make the time to plan and prepare a detailed strategy to follow. Without one you are forced to address only one negotiation objective at a time. Either you pursue objective advantage, at the expense of mutual satisfaction, or you pursue mutual satisfaction, at the expense of objective advantage. And in both outcomes, the negotiation is less than fully successful.

The process of negotiation is the process of discussion, analysis, and bargaining. As such, it involves distinct kinds of purpose and effort in each of these activities:

Discussion—Takes place over interests and issues. It involves the exchange of information and the effort you make to explain your position, to understand another's position, and to set the stage for the analysis and bargaining that follows. Effective discussion aims to build an amicable and cooperative climate so that agreement can be reached more easily. It is positive, stressing the favorable and constructive aspects of our relations with our adversary. It holds out the hope of expanding those relations, of enhancing and enriching areas of common concern. Effective discussion is always an exercise in skillful communication and motivation.

Analysis—Breaks down issues or problems into constituent elements so they can be presented or discussed in terms favorable to our position. Does the customer want faster delivery or earlier completion? Well here are the facts: "To speed up delivery or completion means more manpower or the same manpower working longer hours. This means higher cost to us and higher prices to you."

Is the customer unwilling to pay higher prices? Well here are additional facts: "Speeding up delivery or completion entails the risks of machine or tool breakdowns, labor inefficiency, and quality failures that typically occur under accelerated production schedules."

Analysis is logical, sequential reasoning that relates effects to causes, consequences to actions. It is an exercise in problem solving and persuasion.

Bargaining—The exchange of one objective, issue, or negotiating point for another. It is a trade-off of something you want for something you want more. Bargaining is what negotiation is all about. It is the intrinsic feature of a negotiating process. And those who negotiate must be willing and able to bargain. Bargaining is the medium for exchange in negotiation. The more you get of what you want, and the less you concede to get it, the greater your objective advantage is. The less you get and the more you give up, the less your objective advantage is.

In pursuing advantage, however, you must keep the customer from becoming dissatisfied with the outcome. If he believes he's given too much and gotten too little back, he may act irresponsibly in fulfilling the agreement. He may create problems, terminate the agreement, or try to get even the next time. In the sense that successful negotiation demands that both parties be satisfied with the results, it is a "win-win" concept. In the sense that both parties achieve equal advantage, however, "win-win" is highly unlikely. Attaining objective advantage with mutual satisfaction is a skillful exercise of communication, persuasion, and motivation. It is also a skillful and tactful use of power.

Negotiation is more an art than a science. It is an exercise of intuitive faculties, more like painting or writing poetry than driving a car or building a house. Like art forms, negotiation demands discipline and practice. It is not learned by study; it is learned by doing. Although it has no exact rules, negotiation does employ principles, concepts, and modes of action. And contrary to what the popular literature on negotiation suggests, these are not new or recent discoveries. Negotiation has been a process for resolving differences since the beginning of civilization. And there is a long history of philosophers and statesmen who have observed, practiced, and analyzed the process. Socrates, Machiavelli, Talleyrand, and Benjamin Franklin are just a few who come to mind.

Over 350 years ago, Sir Francis Bacon wrote an essay on negotiation. That essay was annotated by Richard Whately, the Archbishop of Dublin, 200 years later. On the advantages of written over oral negotiation, Bacon wrote the following: "Cunning people can deny anything they said which proves to be disadvantageous. For people who are slippery, there is nothing like writing. . . ." "On the other hand," he continued: "Disagreements will be best prevented by oral communication, for then each man may throw out what occurs to him without being committed in writing to something from which he would be ashamed to draw back. *There is room for mutual explanation, for softening down harsh expressions, for coming to an understanding about common objects which probably are not inconsistent so long as the elements of discord retain the vagueness of spoken words.*"

On the subject of individual versus group negotiations, Bacon said,

> Where you have a number of persons who hold strong prejudices which you wish to break down, you have a much better chance of dealing with them one by one than together, because they keep each other in countenance in holding out against strong reasons to which they can find no answer, and are ashamed each in the presence of the rest to go back from what they have said . . . *but if you untie the faggot, you may break the stitches one by one.*
>
> If on the other hand there are some prevailing prejudices on your side (for example law, ethics, sense of equity) and cool argument would weigh against you, then . . . *you can more easily manage a number of men together than each singly.* . . .

Bacon's comments on dealing with a negotiating adversary are timeless:

Don't push too hard. Prove your point only to what is sufficient to gain acceptance and not more to prove your conclusion. Pushing an argument to extreme absurdity will affront the self-esteem of others, and awaken the disinterest of still others. *People can stand to have their opinion challenged but they will resist the notion that they are fools to believe what they do.* . . .

The best approach (in dealing with a caviller*) is to guard in the first instance against cavils in details and establish that something of such and such a character is desirable; then proceed to settle each of the particular points in detail, one by one . . . *cut a measure into mouthfuls, that it may be the more readily swallowed.*

After one has admitted the desirableness of the end prepared, he should call on the other party to propose the means how that end can be obtained.

You implement a negotiating strategy through negotiating tactics. Like the word strategy, *tactics* derives from a military context. It is simply the techniques or maneuvers you use to achieve the objectives you identified and targeted in your negotiation strategy. To be successful in achieving those objectives you must understand and employ appropriate tactics and be skillful in dealing with the tactics used by your adversary. Most tactics are simple and direct, and readily recognizable to experienced salespeople. Some are more subtle and sophisticated. Following is a summary listing of tactics, with appropriate comments on their use. The list is in no way exhaustive, for no such list could ever be. How can man's ingenuity for pursuing self-interest ever be exhausted?

Establish an atmosphere conducive to agreement. The ultimate goal of negotiation is to agree, not to disagree. Therefore, you should pay attention to the atmosphere surrounding the negotiation. It should be friendly, courteous, and mutually respectful. You should set a proper tone for the meeting—perhaps a statement of common interest and common desire to agree; perhaps a review of your past successful dealings and your hopes for the future. You should emphasize the common advantages to both parties in reaching a mutually acceptable agreement. The more positive the climate, the more smoothly the process will flow.

---

* From the Old English: "One who raises petty or trivial objectives."

Establish an agenda. An agenda is a list of items that will be discussed in the negotiation. Setting an agenda is an important first step of a negotiating process. An agenda provides an orderly basis for considering interests and issues, as well as a restraining device for excluding them from consideration. A well-prepared agenda not only simplifies the process of discussion but may also become a source of advantage to the one who sets it. If you have done your strategy homework well, you should have a clear idea of what you want out of negotiation, in order of importance and in detail. You should also have a clue as to what the buyer or customer wants. Further, you should have a reasonable assessment of strengths and weaknesses in both your position and his. It should be your purpose to structure the agenda so as to (a) further your objectives, (b) capitalize on your strengths, and (c) obscure or offset your weaknesses.

In setting and following an agenda, avoid controversial matters at the outset. Negotiation should proceed along the path of least resistance. Introduce and discuss matters that are easy to agree on. Once you agree on an item or issue put the agreement down in writing. Ask whether your version of the agreement is consistent with the customer's. If it is not, resolve the differences quickly and to mutual satisfaction. If there is no disagreement, go on to the next point, and follow the same procedure. When you reach matters that are controversial, state your desire to reach agreement, but throw the ball to your adversary to explain the problem, present the facts, or propose a solution.

"The first story teller never has a chance." Children play the game of telling tall tales and comparing who can tell the tallest. Clearly, the child who goes first is always at a disadvantage, because his playmates can usually better his best story. In a very real sense, this is also the case in negotiation. Whoever makes the first explanation, gives the first recital of facts, presents the first proposal is vulnerable. He is vulnerable to his own omission of fact, exaggeration of fact, errors of fact. He is vulnerable to proposing what his adversary can claim is "unreasonable" or what his adversary can ridicule as "absurd." In brief, the negotiator who makes the first substantive move toward resolving issues is vulnerable to counterattack or checkmate.

Never make first or arbitrary demands. Negotiation is a process usually taking place between parties having parity or near parity of power. Indeed, if power lies overwhelmingly with one party, little or no negotiation as we know it need occur. The one holding the power can dictate terms as he sees fit. And the agreement, if it can be called that, becomes an imposed agreement. But where there is parity, negotiation is a process of proposing terms, bargaining on terms, and finally reaching agreement. And the general principle to follow is to avoid making first and arbitrary demands. The negotiator who begins with a "final offer" or an "unalterable demand" is simply inviting his adversary's antagonism or his own humiliating retreat.

Probe, listen, probe. The first steps of negotiation should be exploratory. Feel the other party out. Try to determine the real importance of his objectives. What he says he wants and what he would be satisfied in getting are not the same thing. Ask questions that require him to explain, elaborate, fill in details. And then listen. Let him tell you what he understands; what he thinks; what he expects. It is a negotiating fact that the more you learn the better you can assess his and your own true negotiating positions.

Use the power of silence. It is interesting how silence can be intimidating. Let there be a break in the flow of discussion and we begin to feel uneasy. Let us ask a question and receive no immediate response, and we begin to squirm. It's as if we caused the silence and are embarrassed by it.

Many years ago as a young university instructor, I was given some good advice by an old, experienced professor. He told me that "when you ask your students a question and you get no answer, sit back and wait. Count up slowly to thirty and someone will speak up before then. Remember," he said, "silence is more pressing on them than it should be on you. After all, they're causing it!" That's sound teaching advice. It's also sound negotiating advice. Once you've raised a question, wait for an answer. Learn to remain silent. If it was important enough to raise, it's important enough to deserve a response. Don't negate or nullify the thrust of your question by relieving the other party from answering it. If to break the silence you blurt out the first thing that comes to mind, you only weaken your negotiating position. An ambassador for Louis XIV, François de Callieres, once said: "Above all, the good negotiator must possess enough self-control to resist the longing to speak before he has thought what he intends to say."

Introduce trading points early in the negotiation. The benefit of planning a strategy in detail is that you identify your and the customer's objectives in some order of importance. In so doing you can match up specific objectives for potential trade off. For example, you may be willing to trade off a price concession to the customer for a concession in return on quantity or contract period. You may be willing to trade off a quality assurance concession for a price advantage. If you identify an objective or an issue as a trading point—that is, one to be conceded in exchange for another—you must make a case for it. You must make it appear important to you. Things that are given away have little or no worth. Therefore, you argue for trading points. You protest that you cannot surrender them. And then you propose to give up on the item you argued for, for an item you want more. You must not be mechanical in using this tactic. If you're obvious with the tactic and display little subtlety in its practice, you invite being baited by an adversary who merely inflates his original proposals or demands accordingly.

Look for the pattern of concession. The experienced negotiator knows that at some point in the negotiating process a pattern of concession begins to develop. It typically begins on small issues but then proceeds to involve bigger and more important ones. The successful negotiator not only looks for this pattern to begin but also promotes it. He also is careful to keep that pattern from developing within himself.

A pattern of concession can begin at any time and on any issue. A classic illustration is the Paris peace negotiations with North Vietnam. From the very beginning and for days on end, the North Vietnamese argued over the shape of the negotiating table. And then they argued over the color of the baize on the negotiating table. As they gained concessions on these relatively inconsequential items, they became bolder, more assertive, and raised their expectations of what they could gain. As we made concessions, we became less aggressive, less confident, and we lowered our expectations. And so the pattern of concession began.

You promote a pattern of concession when you point out errors, omissions, contradictions, exaggerations in your adversary's position. His admitting that he made a mistake, overlooked a point of fact, or forgot a fact that was relevant are all concessions. They may not be concessions of substance, but the fact that they're made changes both parties' expectations on substantive issues that follow.

Know when to play trumps. In both bridge and pinochle, you don't play trumps while you have higher cards of the same suit being played. The analogy to this principle in negotiating is that we should look at our proposals or demands as a kind of trump. While you can make negotiating points without making proposals or demands of your own, you should do so. For example, every time you point out weaknesses or inconsistencies in the other party's position, you gain negotiating points. And so long as there are further weaknesses or inconsistencies to exploit, there are negotiating points to be gained.

However, a very effective tactic is to let the other party "off the hook" when he is forced to admit weaknesses or inconsistencies. We get him "off the hook" by making a proposal of our own that combines items we argued for earlier but will concede on with items we really want.

> CUSTOMER: I guess you're right. We did tell you to increase production from 100 to 150 units a month, and to buy materials for the balance of the contract.
> SALESPERSON: Well, this is one case where following your instructions is really hurting us. By changing the specifications in midstream we're left with a lot of obsolete inventory. But what's done is done. As to what we do now I would like to propose this: Let's agree to a price of $276.50 on the 800 remaining units. This is about $20.00 a unit more than before. And we'll absorb the costs of the specification change, including the cost of obsolete inventory.

Go with the force. It is important to know the authority or limitations in authority of those with whom we negotiate. It may be poor negotiating tactics to seek a commitment or concession from one who doesn't have the authority to make them. It can cause him to lose face in admitting the fact, or generate animosity where it need not be. Strangely enough, however, not having authority to commit or concede can also be a source of strength. If one is not embarrassed by that fact, his limitation in authority can be a bulwark. As the saying goes, "You can't get blood from a stone!" So, "negotiating" with one who can't commit can be an exercise in futility.

Generally speaking, the higher the authority, the greater the flexibility and room for maneuver are; but, the higher the authority, the greater the expectation to reach agreement alone and quickly. Anyone with a lot of authority is in the limelight and cannot be seen as indecisive, not fully informed, petty, or bickering. For this reason, the higher the authority with whom we negotiate, the stronger our negotiating position can be.

To go with the force is to know the limits and constraints on our adversary. Know them in terms of authority in his organization; but know them also in terms of personal stature, prestige, and emotional strength.

Know the minimum limits of the customer's position, and don't push him too far toward that minimum. Negotiation is a process of give-and-take. You must make concessions to get them. You try to make fewer and less important concessions than you obtain. But, pursuing more and bigger concessions with no regard for the consequences is self-defeating. By pushing an adversary to the point where he can concede no more, you make him hostile, resentful, and anxious to get even. He is not disposed to reach agreement. On the contrary, he wants to frustrate or scuttle it. It is a better tactic to forego an increment of advantage to improve the climate for greater advantage later.

Avoid premature showdowns. One of the elements of a negotiating strategy is a fallback position. If you cannot obtain your initial objective or you meet with solid resistance on an issue or proposal, you must have an avenue of retreat. You must have an alternative position to defend.

It is a poor negotiation tactic to force a decision on an issue when the timing is not right. The decision can only go against you. Thus, to press for a decision when you haven't sold the merits of your position, or when there is serious doubt as to which way the decision will go, invites a showdown. It invites an ultimatum like "take it or leave it." Skillful negotiators may give the impression of being firm and unbending. But they never overplay their hand. In the face of strong opposition, they back away gracefully and defend a new position.

Watch out for the adversary's stacking the cards. The adversary stacks the cards when he does any of the following:

- He introduces past correspondence, reports, memoranda, or cost information into the discussion, all with the aim of weakening your position.
- He cites experts, or brings in experts to support his claims.
- He cites higher authority, or brings in higher authority to confirm or strengthen his position.

If you are on guard against this tactic, you can have documentation of your own that refutes your adversary's position and supports your own. You can bring in your experts or higher authorities to balance the scales. When you do that, however, there is one vital consideration. Make sure that your experts and higher authorities are on your side. (I don't make this point facetiously.) It's distressing how a so-called negotiating team can act like anything but a team. If the team members do not understand and follow a common strategy, if they do not acknowledge a single team leader, if they do not have roles to play that they know and are practiced in playing, then the team is a fiction and a source of weakness. In that case they have stacked the cards against themselves.

Be sensitive to the emotional climate; satisfy emotional needs. Negotiation is a personal process and as such it generates strong emotional crosscurrents. Since the process is in part competitive, it is a battle of wills, a contest of competing skills. Since it also seeks agreement, however, negotiation is also cooperative. And cooperative efforts don't proceed smoothly in a highly charged emotional climate. During negotiation watch out for danger signals like flaring tempers, shouting, or caustic or cutting language. Lower the pressure. Call for a coffee or smoke break. Suggest that both parties caucus. If you're skillful at it, inject a light touch, a pun, a facetious remark. But consider your opposite number carefully. He may take offense at your attitude.

As a personal process, negotiation challenges strong emotional needs. Be fully conscious of your own, and sensitive to those of your adversary. For example:

- Don't lie, resort to bluff, or employ deception. This weakens your self-esteem and keeps you constantly on guard against being found out, which in turn diverts your attention and dissipates your energy.
- Don't size up your adversary in moral, ethical, or sentimental terms. Accept him for what he is and structure your tactics accordingly. Negotiation is not a Sunday School session or a matter of winning the personal regard of your opposite number. You negotiate to gain advantage but also to leave the other party satisfied. Your attitude toward him colors the attitude toward the negotiation itself.
- Avoid saddling your adversary with personal responsibility for problems, difficulties, or misunderstandings. Use the passive tense. Don't say, "you gave us faulty information," but rather, "we received faulty information." Play up the role of the man who isn't there—"they broke the agreement," not "you. . . ." The more personal you make the matter, the more you bring emotions into play. And emotions, like "Russian roulette," can be both unpredictable and dangerous.
- Keep your eyes and ears open. Watch facial expressions, hands, and eyes. Listen for hints of your counterpart's thoughts in his questions, tone of voice, and the direction of his discussion. Be sensitive to his feelings. Flatter him; cajole him; but if the situation demands it, lead him on; bait him; then hook him.

• Last, be calm, cool, and calculating. Don't appear pressed by time or a sense of urgency. Be patient and persevering. Dwight D. Eisenhower once said, "When you are in any contest, you should work as if there were—to the very last minute—a chance to lose it. This is battle, this is politics, this is anything." And "anything" certainly includes negotiation.

Epilogue

Not all value selling situations are negotiating ones. They are not negotiating situations if the following circumstances occur:

1. The customer's requirements are accurately described by his purchase specifications.
2. The customer's specifications are clear, complete, and unambiguous and remain unchanged during the life of the agreement.
3. What the customer specifies and what the seller proposes to supply are the same.
4. The customer's notions of value are consistent with those of the seller, and are not unduly weighted by the competitive price factor alone.
5. There is complete compatibility of objective and interest in the buyer-seller relationship.

Clearly, if all five circumstances are met, there is nothing to negotiate. But merely to recite those circumstances is to highlight how rarely and infrequently they are met. The absence of any single condition warrants negotiation. And in more cases than you might like to believe, all five conditions are absent. Under such circumstances one must negotiate.

A further demand for negotiation stems from the changing nature of industrial markets. They are changing to reflect changing technology, market segmentation, and economic uncertainty. And in the process, the selling function is changing as well. It is changing from an activity that sells features inherent in a product or service to one that creates values and negotiates values as individual customers perceive them.

Item: The rapid pace of technological change is accelerating the pace of product and service innovation. Necessarily, the demands on salespeople to keep abreast of that change are accelerating as well. Salespeople must be not only well-informed about their own technology but also able to relate it effectively to their customer's changing applications. Rather than movers and pushers of products, salespeople are being forced to become solvers of customer problems. And customer problem solving is a negotiating exercise.

Item: Accelerating innovation means shorter life cycles for products and services, from introduction to market to maturity or obsolescence. To salespeople this means less assured repeat business. The time is fast going when the salesperson could close a sale and rest on his laurels. Closing a sale is merely the prelude to discovering and influencing requirements on the next one; negotiating an agreement on the next one. The shorter the cycles, the more repetitive this process is.

Item: Rapid technological change and accelerating innovation have spurred growing market segmentation and customizing. To be better responsive to customer demands, industry is becoming more highly specialized. And in the process the selling function is becoming more oriented to customer concerns. A crude analogy is the difference between selling in a supermarket and selling in a specialty boutique. We take orders in the former; we discuss, analyze, and bargain in the latter.

Item: Increasing competition, particularly from foreign sources, is forcing radical changes in customer buying philosophies and practices. They include:

- Reduction in the number of suppliers in the customer's supply base
- Increasing emphasis on quality assurance—"make it right the first time"
- Increased integration of supplier production and inventory scheduling with actual customer demand—"just-in-time"
- Longer-term agreements with those suppliers who consistently meet quality and time requirements
- Increased emphasis on continuing product development, product improvement, and service support
- Increased emphasis on cost improvement

Given these changes in buying practice, changes in selling practice must follow. Instead of reacting to these developments as time and events unfold, we must negotiate to make them unfold to our advantage.

Item: Economic uncertainty is compounding the risks of doing business today. Volatile market behavior; endemic inflation developing disinflation; high costs of capital; and the implications of high taxes, growing deficits, fluctuating currency, and trade balances all make doing business increasingly fraught with danger. Since selling is what makes business happen, how we sell can increase or mitigate that danger.

A purpose of negotiation is to identify risks, analyze their consequences, and arrive at agreements that avoid them, lessen them, or allocate them advantageously.

The concept of value selling is a rationale for selling effectively in today's evolving markets.

- It is correctly oriented to the customer and his product, process, and marketing requirements.
- It is firmly and substantively based on the relating of our product or service features and capabilities to those requirements.
- It is realistically conscious of the need to be cost-effective in meshing or matching the two.

And given the uncertainties, risks, and inevitable differences in buyer-seller perceptions, selling value is negotiating for value.

Index

Italics refer to tables and figures.

accounting system
  buying and selling value in,
    34–35
  direct costs in, 28–30
  indirect costs in, 29
  material costs in, 30
acquisition costs, 41–43, 51
actual costs, 48
administration, 80
after-sale service, 78–79
agenda, establishment of, 203
agreement, establishment of
    atmosphere conducive to,
    202
allocation, of overhead, 50–51
amortization, 49
answer file, 119–120

appropriations
  lack of, 122
  request for, 33–34
arguments, avoidance of, 129
assembly controls, 78
attitudes, in negotiations,
    193–194
authority
  purchasing, 18–26
  recourse to, 192–193
authorization, 6–7
auto expenses, 49
automotive industry, suppliers
    for, 169–170
availability
  capabilities, 79–80
  categories of, costs of, 41–47

availability *(continued)*
   costs of, 41–42, 51
   requirements of, 36–37
   of reseller, costs of, 63

Bacon, Sir Francis, on
   negotiation, 201–202
bargaining, 200
bids, with services broken out,
   167
bottom line assessment, 89
bridging statements, 119–120
budgets
   as constraints on spending,
   125
   planning of, 70
buyer
   buying influences on, *22–25*
   types of, 20–21, *22–25*
   see also buying influences;
     customer
buyer-seller relationship,
   compatibility in, 211
buying decision, value
   contribution factors in,
   72–73
buying influences, 9–10
   definition of, 13–14, 171
   at design stage, 65
   identification and
     responsiveness to, 95
   knowledge of, 149
   knowledge of how and when
     to apply sales effort with,
     150
   meaningful, 125
   objections raised by, 112–113
   of purchasing authority,
     18–26
   by type of buyer, *22–25*
   types of, 18

value perceptions of, 12–26,
   92
value selling presentation and,
   94
see also customer

capital investment
   appropriate requests for,
   33–34
   imputed costs and, 36
capitalize on objection technique,
   117–118
cash flow
   discounted, 33
   value in exchange and, 173
change
   customer-initiated, 110–111
   handling of, customer-initiated,
   132–138
   technological, 212
clerical costs, 42
commitments, failure to honor,
   146
commodities, 16
commodity suppliers, computer
   systems in evaluation of,
   166–167
competition
   assessment of, 150
   demands of, 53
   evaluation of, 73
   from foreign sources, 212–213
   of Japanese companies,
   168–169
   in negotiation, 188, 190
competition-imposed demands,
   91
complaints
   analysis of, 127–128
   definition of, 110, 126–127
   excuses for, 129–130
   handling of, 126–129

lingering of, 130
listening to, 129
as opportunities, 127
principles for handling of,
129–132
proposal of solutions to,
111–112
scenarios of, 130–132
search for solutions to, 128
solutions to, 128–129
computer-assisted machines, 78
concession, pattern of, 205
consensus evaluation, 155–157
consignment, 44
consumer needs, 53
control capabilities, 79–80
conventions, 192
correction costs, *see* failure
correction costs
cost, 2
accounting, 48
accounting view of, 28–35
of acquisition, 42–43
actual versus standard, 48
availability, 51
as common element in value
perception, 92–93
of defect or failure correction,
39–42
of defect or failure detection,
39
of defect or failure prevention,
37–38
definitions of, 48–49
definitions of lowest, 172
of depletion and delivery
delays, 45–47
direct, 28–29, 48
of ensuring quality, 37–47
fixed, 33, 51
importance of, 28
imputed, 35–36, 51

incremental, 51
indirect, 29, 49
meaning of and relationship to
value, 27–47
nonaccounting view of, 35–36
opportunity, 52
overhead, 49–51
of possession, 43–45
purchases resulting in fixed,
33–34
quality, 52
of reseller, 63–64
of satisfying purchase
requirements, 36–47
semi-variable, 31, 52
start-up, 52
total, 34
unit, 49
variable, 31–32, 52
variable versus fixed, 30–31
variance of, 49
ways to identify, 51–52
see also cost-effectiveness; price
cost-accounting definitions,
48–52
cost avoidance, 107
cost-effectiveness
establishment of to customer,
96–97, 101–103, 105–106
product/service features and,
93
real meaning of, 60
related to end user's
requirements, 70
in relation to customer's
requirements, 68
value contributions and, 75
value selling checklist to show,
87–89
cost offsets, 107–108
cost savings, 107
credibility, 139–141

credibility*(continued)*
  of company as supplier,
    139–140, 154–170
  of salesperson, 141–148,
    149–154
customer
  ability to help or hurt,
    190–191
  as adversary, 184
  assessment of practices and
    preferences of, 149
  buying influences on, 60
  combination, 15
  concentration of costs of, 61
  consumer-buyer versus
    industrial-institutional, 9–10
  correct assessment of,
    149–151
  cost of calls on, 12
  definition of, ix, 171
  dissatisfactions of, 126–132
  evaluation of information
    inquiries of, 150
  external factors impinging on,
    3
  factors that influence, 9–10
  failure to recognize changing
    priorities of, 147–148
  keeping informed, 154
  knowledge of, 59–61
  long-term versus short-term
    behavior and priorities of,
    149–150
  loss of business by, 126
  marketing and distribution
    processes of, 62
  product categories of, 15–17
  product/service uses of, 61
  quantity and time
    requirements of, 61
  requirements of, ix
  and salesperson, 140–141

  types of, 14–15
  understanding of business of,
    143
  variations in motivation of,
    14–15
  visible buying influence of,
    10
  see also buyer; buying
    influences; customer
    requirements
customer constraints, 81
customer-initiated changes,
    110–111
  assessment of, 138
  effects of, 132–133
  exploitation of, 133–135
  handling of, 132–138
  important considerations in
    dealing with, 137–138
  as opportunities, 135–136,
    138
  as service, 133–135
customer order processing, 80
customer policies, assessment of,
    149
customer requirements, 3
  anticipation of, 149
  capabilities to meet, 76–77
  careful reading of, 153
  consumer versus industrial,
    53–54
  cost-effective satisfaction of,
    87, 89
  day-to-day versus investment
    purchases, 58
  definition of, 172
  demands interpreted as,
    91–92
  demonstration of how
    product/service features
    satisfy, 96–100
  as derived requirements, 91

of end user, 68–70
focus on, 59–61
harmonizing of with supplier's
  interests, 151–153
implied in specifications, 76
of industrial customer, 6–7
and influencing of,
  identification of, 53–70
and interpretation of demands
  on, identification of, 54–55
as obstacle to sale, 121
of OEMs, 64–68
problem- or opportunity-
  derived, 57–58
product/service features related
  to, 75
quantity and time, 8
and responsiveness to,
  identification of, 95
satisfaction of, 54
specifications of, 7–8
specifier of, 8
supplier capabilities and,
  78–80
understanding of, 142–143
customer satisfaction, ensurance
  of, 153–154
customer training, 164–165
customs, 192

data capturing procedures, 78
decentralized operations,
  purchasing authority in, 19
deception, 208
defect correction costs, 39–41,
  52
defect detection costs, 39, 52
defect prevention costs, 37–38,
  52
delivery
  categories of costs of, 41–47
  costs of, 41–42

definition of, 158
delays in, costs of, 42, 45–47
measurement of, 159
performance, 162
requirement for, 36–37
reseller, costs of, 63
demands, as requirements,
  91–92
depletion costs, 42, 45–47, 51
depreciation, 49
derived requirements, 91
design engineer, 7
  value to, 27
details, lack of attention to, 144
detection costs, see failure
  detection costs
direct costs, 28–29
  definition of, 48
  identification of, 30
  as variable, 31–32
direct labor costs, 48
discounted cash flow, 33
distribution, premium costs of,
  45
downtime, costs of, 45
dues, 49
duty, sense of, 193

economic conditions, 189–190
economic uncertainty, 213
emotional needs, 208–209
end-user customer
  evaluation of specifications of,
    70
  problems in identifying
    requirements of, 57–58
  process demands and, 56–57
  requirements of, 56–57
  selling to, 68–70
end-user markets, 15
engineering change, 126
engineering controls, 77

engineering services, 77
esteem value, 1
  in industrial sales situations, 3
expectations, of buyer and seller,
    193
expense classifications, 50

fabrication controls, 78
facilities, capacity and, 79
failure correction costs, 39–41,
    52
failure detection costs, 39, 52
failure prevention costs, 37–38,
    52
federal government, 6
feedback, lack of, 112
fixed-cost items, 33
  purchasing process for, 33–34
fixed costs, 30–31, 51
  buying of items, 33–34
follow-up, 144–145
foreign competition, 212–213
function, 3
  basic and secondary, 4
  definition of, 4

goodwill, loss of, 45

imputed costs, 35–36, 51
incremental costs, 51
index rating systems, 160–170
  shortcomings of, 162–164
  theory behind, 161–162
indirect costs, 29, 49
industrial demand
  increased volatility of, 13–14
  market categories and, 14–15
industrial-institutional buyer
  buying procedures of, 5–6
  factors influencing, 9–10
  meaning of value to, 1–11
industrial market

changes in, 13
changing nature of, 212–213
industrial requirements, 53–54
information
  meaningful and timely, 144
  for negotiations, 198–199
  as source of power, 191
information systems, 78
innovation, acceleration of, 212
inspection controls, 78
institutional buyers, *see* industrial-
    institutional buyer
inventories
  controls on, 80
  costs of, 43–45
investment, interest on, 35
Ison's Law of Ten, 41n

Japanese competition, 168–169
just-in-time controls, 46

labor, direct costs of, 48
legal considerations, 81

maintenance materials, 50
make and hold, 44
management, buying influence
    of, 21, 23, *25, 26*
manufacturing
  costs of defective material to,
    40
  premium costs of, 45
  processes of, 77–78
manufacturing overhead, 49
  allocation of, 50–51
  non-labor expenses in, 49–50
market categories, 14–15
market environment, demands
    of, 53, 91
marketing, design and, 65
market share, 172–173
materials

direct costs of, 48
obsolescence of, 50
membership costs, 49
Miles, Larry, and value analysis, 4

negotiating position, correctness of, 191–192
negotiations, 171–174
  agenda for, 203
  aims of, 180
  analysis of problem in, 200
  bargaining in, 200
  case examples of, 175–179
  circumstances that prohibit, 211–212
  competition and, 174
  competitiveness of, 188
  cultural conditioning against, 181–182
  customer's minimum limits in, 207
  definition of, 173–174
  demand for, 212
  development of positive attitude toward, 182–183
  development of strategy for, 183–194, *see also* negotiation strategy
  discussion in, 199–200
  effective, 174–183
  emotional climate in, 208–209
  first or arbitrary demands in, 203–204
  going with force in, 206
  historic perspectives on, 201–202
  information needed for, 198–199
  pattern of concession in, 205
  power in, 188–189

premature showdowns in, 207
  process of, 180–181
  purpose of, 213
  reasons for need for, 212–213
  site for, 198
  skills for, 199
  stacking cards in, 207–208
  strategy worksheet for, 194–209
  tactics for, 202–209
  trading points in, 204–205
  when to play trumps in, 205–206
  when to start, 198
negotiation strategy
  action plan in, 195
  functions of, 184–185
  identification of objectives in, 186–188
  objective setting in, 185–186
  sources of power in, 189–194
  team approach to, 198
  worksheet for, 194–209
nonmanufacturing overhead, 51

objections
  analysis of, 116
  answer file for, 119–120
  anticipation of, 109
  bridging statements and handling of, 119–120
  capitalizing on, 117–118
  direct answer to, 114–115
  evasion of, 115–116
  handling of, 112–114
  implications of, 119
  as opportunity in disguise, 109–110
  petty or irrelevant, 113
  questioning of, 116–117
  during sales presentation, 111

objections *(continued)*
  techniques for handling of,
    114–118
  versus obstacles, 123–124
obligation, sense of, 193
obsolescence, 50
obstacles
  elimination of, 120–126
  nullification of basic cause of,
    124–125
  unexpected, 125–126
occupancy expense, 50
OEM, *see* original equipment
  manufacturers (OEMs)
office supplies, 50
one-time purchase, determination
  of requirements for, 69
operations manager, 122
opportunity costs, 35–36, 52
original equipment manufacturers
  (OEMs), 15
  influences on sales to, 56
  influencing definition of
    requirements of, 66–68
  selling to, 64–66
  technical requirements of, 64
overhead costs, 29, 49
  allocation of manufacturing,
    50–51
  manufacturing, 49
  non-labor expenses in
    manufacturing, 49–50
  nonmanufacturing, 51

packaging, 72
  controls of, 78
packing controls, 78
payback analysis, 33
performance
  definition of, 162
  rating of, 161, *see also*
    suppliers, rating systems for
personal attitudes, 193–194

planning costs, 42
plant closing, 126
policies, failure to comply with,
  146–147
positive attitude, 152–153
possession costs, 41, 43–45, 51
  reduction of, 44, 46
postage expense, 50
power, 188–189
  sources of, 189–194
precedents, 192
premium costs
  with defective materials, 40
  of manufacture and
    distribution, 45
premium inspection, cost of,
  39–40
prevention costs, *see* failure
  prevention costs
price, 2
  competitiveness in, 168
  definition of, 157
  measurement of, *159*
  profit and loss and, 29–30
  quality and, 40–41
  reasonable, 172
  see also cost
price performance, 162–163
problem analysis, 116
  in negotiations, 200
procedures, failure to comply
  with, 146–147
process engineering, 55
process-imposed demands, 91
  and end-user customer
    requirements, 56–57
process improvements,
  opportunities for, 57–58
procurement controls, 78
procurement procedure, 5–7
  increased formalization of,
    13–14
product

buying decision of, 72–73
categories of, 15–17
demands of, 53
design of, 64–65
engineering of, 55–56
features and customer
    requirements of, 96–105
function of, 66–67, 69
improvement of, 79
knowledge of, 142, 154
specialty, 16
value contribution of, features,
    74–76
value of, to customer, 66–68
product engineer, responsibilities
    of, 123
product-imposed demands, 91
production capacity, 79
production engineering activities,
    55–56
production manager, value to,
    28
production planning, 79–80
production process, 53
productivity standards, 78
profitability, 173
profit/loss relationship, 29–30
program management, 80
protocol, failure to comply with,
    146–147
purchase requirements
    costs of satisfying, 36–47
    definition of, 36
    demands interpreted as,
        91–92
    as derived requirements, 91
    determination of, 55
    process demands and, 56–57
    see also customer requirements
purchase specifications, 56
purchasing, authority for, 18–26
    in decentralized operations, 19
    see also purchasing agent

purchasing agent
    buying influence of, 10, *22,
        24*
    function of, 9
    increased influence of, 21
    limits of authority of, 122
    professionalization of, 21
    strength of buying influence
        of, 19–20
    value to, 27
    see also buying influences
purchasing requirements
    by customer type, 59
    day-to-day versus investment,
        58
    problem- and opportunity-
        derived, 57–58
    see also customer requirements

quality
    controls of, 78
    costs of ensuring, 37–47, 52
    definition of, 157
    measurement of, *158*
    performance, 162
    requirements, 36
quality-assurance related
        capabilities, 77–79
quantity requirements, 8
questioning objection technique,
    116–117

rate-of-return analysis, 33–34
raw material controls, 78
rejection costs, 39
reliability engineering, 78
reputation, 80–81
requirements-cost relationship, 72
    see also cost; customer
        requirements; purchasing
        requirements
requisition, 8–9
resale markets, 15

reseller
  costs of, 63–64
  function of, 63
  selling to, 61–64
resource management, 54
risks, identification of, 213

sale
  closing, viii
  customer satisfaction and,
    153–154
  failure to follow through on,
    144–145
  loss of, 45–46
  technical specialists to help
    close, 151
salesperson
  assessment of customer and
    sales situation by, 149–151
  causes of dissatisfaction with,
    140–141
  closing loop from sale to
    customer satisfaction by,
    153–154
  credibility of, 141–148
  harmonizing customer
    requirements and interests
    of employers by, 151–153
  role of, 140–141
  skills of, 148–149
sales resistance, elimination of,
  120–126
sales situation, correct assessment
  of, 149–151
sampling methods, 78
scaling up, benefits of, 67
scheduling time costs, 42
selling, cost-justifying, 11
selling up
  seeking opportunities for, 151
  support and cooperation in,
    152

selling value, requirements
    determination process for,
    61–62
semi-variable costs, 31, 52
service, 16–17
  categories of, 15–17
  customer changes and,
    133–135
  importance of, 110
  knowledge of, 142
shipping controls, 78
silence, power of, 204
skills, in negotiations, 193–194,
  199
specialty products, 16
specifications, 7
  constraints on, 64–65
  influences on, 56, 64–65
  of systems versus product, 67
specifiers, buying influence of,
  20, 22, 24, 26
standard costs, 48
start-up costs, 52
statistical process controls, 78
stock control, 78
stockouts, 45
storage costs, 43–44
strategy
  checklist for, 71–89
  definition of, 183–184
suppliers
  for automotive industry,
    169–170
  availability, 79–80
  computer systems in evaluation
    of performance, 164,
    166–167
  consensus evaluation of,
    155–157
  credibility of, 139–140
  critical nature of product of,
    190–191

differences in capabilities of, 76–77
index rating evaluation of, 160–170
performance of, 155
quality-assurance-related capabilities of, 77–79
rating systems for, 155–170, *see also specific systems*
salesperson's knowledge and representation of, 150
selection of, 9
uniqueness or exclusivity of offerings of, 190
weakness in rating systems for, 163
weighted-point system evaluation of, 157–160
what purchasing managers want from, 169, *170*
see also supplier service
supplier service, 164
customer failure to acknowledge, 166–167
separate quotation of, 167–168
value contribution of, 164–165
support service, 78–79
systems, 17
systems contracting, 44
systems specification, 67

technical services, 164–165
technical specialists, to help close sale, 151
technological change, rapid pace of, 212
time factor, 191
time requirements, 8
tooling control, 77
trading points, 204–205

traffic capabilities, 80
transportation capabilities, 80
travel expenses, 50
tuitions, 49

unit costs, 49
users
buying influences of, 20–21, 23, 25, 26
failure to follow up on, 145
utilities, 50

value
to buyers, 2
and buying influences, perceptions of, 92
of direct material cost, perceptions of, 30
in exchange, 1, 172–173
meaning of to industrial customer, 1–11
negotiating for, 171–209
perceptions of, 2–3, 90–91
as reflection of buying influences' interests and objectives, 27–28
selling of, 34–35
shifting of perceptions of, 13
shifting priorities in perceptions of, 14
standardization of, 1–2
in use, 1, 3, 5
vagueness of, vii
see also value analysis; value contributions
value analysis, 3–11
technique of, 66
value analysis-value engineering, 4–5
value contributions
acknowledged, 72
competitive evaluation and, 74

value contributions *(continued)*
  cost benefits and, 75
  customer views of, 72–73
  definition of, 71
  perception of, 71–72
  product/service features and, 74
  of supplier service, 164–165
value-cost relationship, 73–74
value engineering, 4–5
value offsets, 173
value selling
  basic premise of, 171
  bottom line assessment of, 89
  cost-accounting definitions for, 48–52
  establishment of credibility in, 139–170
  opportunities for, 58–61
  see also value; value contributions
Value Selling Checklist, *82–86*

how to use, 86–88
Value Selling Presentation, 90
  objective of, *93*
  premises of, 90–93
  preparation of, 94–108
variable costs, 30, 52
  as direct cost, 31–32
variances, 49

warranties, 79
weighted point, 158
weighted-point evaluation system, 157–160
  composite rating of, *160*
  factor evaluation guide for, *160*
  shortcomings of, 162
  theory behind, 161–162
Whately, Richard, on negotiation, 201
win-win agreements, 173